The Self-Sabotage Syndrome

Adult Children In The Workplace

Janet Geringer Woititz, Ed.D.

Health Communications, Inc.
Deerfield Beach, Florida

Library of Congress Cataloging-in-Publication Data

Woititz, Janet Geringer.
 The self-sabotage syndrome / Janet Geringer Woititz.
  p.   cm.
 Bibliography: p.
 ISBN 1-55874-050-3
  1. Alcoholism and employment. 2. Adult children of alcoholics-
 -Employment. 3. Adult children of alcoholics — Psychology.
 I. Title.
 HF5549.5.A4W66   1989   89-11031
 362.2'923—dc20   CIP

Published by: Health Communications, Inc.
        3201 S.W. 15th Street
        Deerfield Beach, Florida 33442

ACKNOWLEDGMENTS

The impact of growing up in a dysfunctional family is experienced in every aspect of adult life. The workplace is no exception.

In order to demonstrate the ways in which the work environment becomes a home away from home, I drew on both my own clinical experience and that of a number of colleagues. I acknowledge the assistance of the following consultants:

Chapters 9 and 10 draw heavily on conversations with Mel Sandler, M.S.W. Mel is Managing Director of the Institute for Counseling and Training, West Caldwell, New Jersey. His career includes extensive involvement in workplace settings, counseling employees and training management personnel to deal with employees with personal problems. Settings in which he has worked include United Airlines; The American Federation of State, County, and Municipal Employees; and The International Ladies' Garment Workers' Union. He currently acts as a consultant in corporate workplace settings.

Other chapters benefited from the input of:

Administrative

Gyni Garner, M.S.W. — Charlotte, North Carolina

Bob Lynn, N.C.C., C.A.C. — Piscataway, New Jersey

Kerry Peltier, M.A., C.A.C. — Verona, New Jersey

Professional

Pat Clyne, B.A., R.N. — Astoria, New York

Kathi Goode, M.A. — Montclair, New Jersey

Rev. James Mahoney, Ph.D. — Chatham, New Jersey

Audrey Roberts, M.A. — Montclair, New Jersey

Clinical

George Brines, A.A.S., C.A.C. — Lafayette, Indiana

Dana Finnegan, Ph.D. — South Orange, New Jersey

Emily McNally, M.A. — New York, New York

Martha Moore-Russell, Ph.D. — Princeton, New Jersey

Amy Stromsten, C.A.C. — Cambridge, Massachusetts

Bick Wanck, M.D. — Conifer Park, New York

Research

Coleen Peruo, B.A. — East Rutherford, New Jersey

Patrick Peruo, Ph.D. — East Rutherford, New Jersey

General

Jackson Braider, M.A. — New York, New York

Ed Gogek, M.D. — Providence, Rhode Island

Matt Johnson, B.S.W. — Anchorage, Alaska

Marilyn Stager — Hawthorne, New Jersey

Lisa Woititz, B.A. — Montclair, New Jersey

Employee Assistance Programs

Debby Bern, M.S.W. — New Rochelle, New York

Leighton Clark, M.S.W. — Chicago, Illinois

Betty-Ann Weinstein, M.S.W. — Washington, D.C.

To my family at work who have demonstrated that caring, awareness, hard work and commitment make a healthy environment possible.

And to my family at home who have demonstrated that caring, awareness, hard work and commitment make a healthy environment possible.

CONTENTS

PREFACE

hen I wrote the book *Adult Children Of Alcoholics*, it was with children of alcoholics in mind. Since its publication in 1983, it has become clear that what is true for children of alcoholics is just as true for children growing up in other types of dysfunctional families. If you did not grow up with alcoholism, but lived, for example, with other compulsive behaviors, such as gambling, drug abuse or overeating, experienced chronic illness, profound religious attitudes, were adopted, lived in foster care or in other potentially dysfunctional systems, there is a good chance that you will identify with the characteristics described for adult children of alcoholics.

That is why I have used the term Adult Children in the title of this book without being more specific. The term Adult Children has come to indicate those adults who grew up in a variety of dysfunctional families and need to improve the relationship they have with the child part of themselves. This problematic relationship causes difficulty in all aspects of their lives. The workplace is no exception. The cluster of symptoms that relate to difficulties in the workplace is described in this book (formerly titled *Home Away From Home*). I define these symptoms as the Self-Sabotage Syndrome.

Janet G. Woititz

INTRODUCTION

The impact of growing up with alcoholism pervades every aspect of adult life. It influences feelings of self, relationships and one's ability to get things done, regardless of whether one is looking at the home, social, or work environment.

Since a large portion of one's waking hours is spent in the workplace, the way one feels and behaves in that environment, whatever or wherever that setting may be, is a significant part of one's life.

The same dynamics that cause difficulty at home may serve one in very good stead in the workplace: A secretary's family may go nuts with her compulsive need for order and attention to detail, but her boss probably values it greatly. Your friend may be very grateful that you are driving him to work while his car is in the shop, but your supervisor may see your lateness as a hostile act.

Similar traits manifest themselves differently depending on the environment. These examples of issues — issues involving control of environment as a reaction to growing up with anarchy and the inability to say no for fear of rejection — are fairly common to children of alcoholics. This study evolved in order to satisfy my own curiosity as to how these issues play out in the workplace.

Regardless of the degree of success that you achieve in the world of work, if you are an ACoA, there are questions that continue to plague you. These are the result of feelings that get in the way of your finding the satisfaction appropriate to your job performance or finding the courage either to assert your needs or make necessary changes. This is not only confusing to you but damaging to your self-image. You end up very angry at yourself. "Why do I . . . when I know better? Why don't I . . . when I know how? Why can't I accept praise? Why does criticism devastate me? Why do I sabotage success? Why am I overwhelmed so much of the time? Why is everyone else better able to cope than I? Is there any end to it? Could my parents really be responsible?" And on and on this seemingly endless list of questions goes.

Adult children of alcoholics (ACoAs) are among any company's most productive and valuable employees. You will find them in high management positions as well as in unskilled jobs. They are dedicated, conscientious, capable, loyal and will do everything in their power to please. These qualities are brought to whatever they do regardless of status or pay scale.

If ACoAs are so desirable as employees, what are their problems? One goal of this book is to encourage Employee Assistance Programs (EAPs) to pay particular attention to addressing them.

1. ACoAs are prime candidates for burnout. The excellent performance you admire and want has a limited life span.
2. ACoAs tend not to know how to handle stress and lose more days due to illness than other employees.
3. ACoAs are prone to depression, especially around holiday time, so performance may lag at those times.
4. ACoAs have difficulty with separation and change so are prone to quit impulsively or do poorly with new opportunities.
5. ACoAs run a higher risk of developing their own substance-abuse problems than other employees.

Enlightened Employee Assistance Program personnel are able to identify children of alcoholics' issues when they surface and as a result are able to treat many right in the workplace. More and more EAP programs are reporting that large numbers of their caseloads are children of alcoholics. Early intervention with children of alcoholics in the workplace is cost-effective.

Models developed for identifying and treating children of alcoholics may be applied to children from other dysfunctional families as well. Many similarities exist between ACoAs and those who grew up with other compulsive behaviors such as gambling, drug abuse, and overeating; those who experienced chronic illness or those who were subjected to extreme fundamentalist religious attitudes. Compulsive behaviors can also be seen in those who were adopted or lived in foster care. The patterns are not exclusive so the benefits of workplace awareness carry even greater significance.

This book is designed to answer questions for the ACoA employee and to develop a perspective for EAP personnel to include in designing their programs. The goal is to make the work experience more satisfying for the person who has grown up in a dysfunctional system and make the work environment more effective for all concerned. Samples of different work environments and how they reflect the old life at home are included. How and why these set up a work environment that is all too reminiscent of the family of origin becomes clear.

Also included are the myths held by ACoAs in the workplace and how these perpetuate a poor self-image — leading to work-aholism, subsequent burnout and the inability of many ever to get started at all.

The toxic interaction of these elements among peers and supervisors — the inevitability of it — will become apparent.

Ways to affect change from the point of view of the counselor, the ACoA and the corporation are dealt with in the second half of the book. It is designed to be used by the employee for self-help and by the Employee Assistance person as a counseling tool.

PART ONE

ACoAs
On The Job

1
The Overview

dult children of alcoholics have a number of characteristics in common. And regardless of the kind of work they do, whether they are bookkeepers or bus drivers, librarians or lawyers, they bring these characteristics with them into the workplace.

Adult Children Of Alcoholics
Guess At What Normal Is

The significance of this statement cannot be overestimated, as it is the ACoA's most profound characteristic. Adult children of alcoholics simply have no experience with what is normal. If you are an ACoA, you will recognize what we're talking about here.

After all, when you take a look at your history, how could you have any understanding of normalcy? Your home life varied from slightly mad to extremely bizarre.

Since this was the only home life you knew, what others would consider "slightly mad" or "extremely bizarre" were usual to you. If there was an occasional day that one could characterize as

3

"normal," it certainly was not typical and therefore could not have had much meaning.

Beyond your chaotic day-to-day life, part of what you did was to live in fantasy. You lived in a world that you created, a world all your own, a world of what life would be like *if* . . . what your home would be like *if* . . . the way your parents would relate to each other *if* . . . the things that would be possible for you *if* . . . And you structured a whole life based on something that probably was impossible. The unrealistic fantasies about what life would be like if your parent got sober probably helped you survive, but they added to your confusion as well.

You have no frame of reference for what it is like to be in a normal household. You also have no frame of reference for what is okay to say and to feel. In a family that is not dysfunctional, one does not have to walk on eggs all the time. One doesn't have to question or repress one's feelings all the time. Because you did have to be careful, you became confused. Many things from the past contributed to your having to guess at what normal is.

What this means in the workplace is that ACoAs . . .

1. Are ideal candidates for exploitation because they don't know when to say no.
2. Very frequently become scapegoats because they ask a million questions.
3. Will pick inappropriate role models because they make assumptions and don't check them out.

Adult Children Of Alcoholics Have Difficulty In Following A Project Through From Beginning To End

The topic one evening in an Adult Children of Alcoholics' meeting was procrastination. When I asked the group members to talk about what it meant to them, the opening response was either, "I'm the world's biggest procrastinator," or "Somehow I just don't seem to be able to finish anything that I start."

These comments are fairly typical and it's not too hard to understand why a difficulty exists. ACoAs are not procrastinators in the usual sense. The great job was always around the corner. The big deal was always about to be made. The work that needed to be done around the house would be done in no time . . . The toy that will be built . . . the go-cart . . . the doll house . . . and on and on.

I'm going to do this. I'm going to do that. But this or that never really happened. Not only didn't it happen, but the alcoholic wanted credit simply for having the idea, even for intending to do it. You grew up in this environment. There were many wonderful ideas but they were never acted on. If they were, so much time passed that you had forgotten about the original idea.

Who took the time to sit down with you when you had an idea for a project and said, "That's a good idea. How are you going to go about doing it? How long is it going to take you? What are the steps involved?" Probably no one. When was it that one of your parents said, "Gee, that idea is terrific! You sure you can do it? Can you break it down into smaller pieces? Can you make it manageable?" Probably never.

This is not to suggest that all parents who do not live with alcohol teach their children how to solve problems. But it is to suggest that in a functional family the child has this behavior and attitude as a model. The child observes the process and may even ask questions along the way. The learning may be more indirect than direct but it is present. Since your experience was so vastly different, it should be no surprise that you have a problem with following a project through from beginning to end. You haven't seen it happen and you don't know how to make it happen. Lack of knowledge isn't the same as procrastination.

What this means in the workplace is that ACoAs . . .

1. Are shortsighted.
2. Will operate superbly under pressure.
3. Will be unable to complete long-term projects.

Adult Children Of Alcoholics Lie When It Would Be Just As Easy To Tell The Truth

Lying is basic to the family system affected by alcohol. It masquerades in part as overt denial of unpleasant realities, cover-ups, broken promises and inconsistencies. It takes many forms and has many implications. Although it is somewhat different from the kind of lying usually talked about, it certainly is a departure from the truth.

The first and most basic lie is the family's denial of the problem, so the pretense that everything at home is in order is a lie and the family rarely discusses the truth openly, even with each other.

Perhaps somewhere in one's private thoughts there is a recognition of the truth, but there is also the struggle to deny it.

The next lie, the cover-up, relates to the first one. The nonalcoholic family member covers up for the alcoholic member. As a child, you saw your nonalcoholic parent covering up for your alcoholic parent. You heard him or her on the phone making excuses for your mother or father for not fulfilling an obligation, not being on time. That's part of the lie that you lived.

You also heard a lot of promises from your alcoholic parent. These, too, turned out to be lies.

Lying as the norm in your house became part of what you knew and what could be useful to you. At times, it made life much more comfortable. If you lied about getting your work done, you could get away with being lazy for a while. If you lied about why you couldn't bring a friend home or why you were late coming home, you could avert unpleasantness. It seemed to make life simpler for everybody.

Lying has become a habit. That's why the statement, "Adult children of alcoholics lie when it would be just as easy to tell the truth" is relevant. But if lying is what comes naturally, perhaps it is not as easy to tell the truth.

In this context, "It would be just as easy to tell the truth," means that you derive no real benefit from lying.

What this means in the workplace is that ACoAs . . .

1. Second-guess the person who asks so that they can give the answer they *think* the person wants.
2. Will agree to perform tasks they cannot perform because they assume that they *should* be able to do them or they would not have been asked.

Adult Children Of Alcoholics Judge Themselves Without Mercy

When you were a child, there was no way that you could be good enough. You were constantly criticized. You believed that your family would be better off without you because you believed you were the cause of the trouble. You may have been criticized for things that made no sense. "If you weren't such a rotten kid, I wouldn't have to drink." It makes no sense, but if you hear something often enough, for a long enough period of time, you will end up believing it. As a result, you internalized these criticisms as negative self-feelings. They remain, even though no one is saying them to you anymore.

Since there is no way for you to meet the standards of perfection that you have internalized from childhood, you are always falling short of the mark you have set for yourself. When you were a child, whatever you did was not quite good enough. No matter how hard you tried, you should have tried harder. If you got an A, it should have been an A+. You were never good enough. A client told me that his mother was so demanding that when he was in basic training, he found the sergeants loose. So perfectionism became a part of you, who you are, a part of the way you see yourself. The "shoulds" and "should nots" can become paralyzing after a while.

Your judgment of others is not nearly as harsh as your judgment of yourself, although it is hard for you to see other people's behavior in terms of a continuum either. Black and white, good or bad, are typically the way you look at things. Either side is an awesome responsibility. You know what it feels like to be bad and how those feelings make you behave. And then if you are good, there is always the risk that it won't last. So either way, you set yourself up. Either way there is a great amount of pressure on you all of the time. How difficult and stressful life is. How hard it is to just sit back and relax and say, "It's OK to be me."

What this means in the workplace is that ACoAs . . .

1. Will assume that they are responsible for anything that goes wrong.
2. Will not accept strokes if the task was easy to accomplish.
3. Will downplay any credit they receive for completing a difficult task because "It's all a part of the job."

Adult Children Of Alcoholics Have Difficulty Having Fun; They Take Themselves Very Seriously

These two characteristics are very closely linked. If you're having trouble having fun, you're probably taking yourself very seriously and if you don't take yourself all that seriously, chances are you can have fun.

Once again, in order to understand this problem you need to look back at your childhood. How much fun was your childhood? You don't have to answer that. Children of alcoholics simply don't have much fun. One child of an alcoholic described it as "chronic trauma." You didn't hear your parents laughing and joking and fooling around. Life was a very serious, angry business. You didn't really learn to play with the other kids. You could join in some of the games but were you really able to let yourself go and have fun? Even if you could have, it was discouraged. The tone around the house put a damper on your fun. Eventually, you just went along with everyone else. Having fun just wasn't fun. There was no place for it in your house. You gave it up. It just wasn't a workable idea. The spontaneous child within was squashed.

Having fun, being silly, being childlike, is to be foolish. It is no wonder that adult children of alcoholics have difficulty having fun. Life is too serious.

You also have trouble separating yourself from your work, so you take yourself very seriously at whatever job you have to do. You can't take the work seriously and not take yourself seriously. You are therefore a prime candidate for burnout.

One night a client turned to me with a very angry face and said, "You may make me laugh at myself but I want you to know I don't think it's funny."

What this means in the workplace is that for the ACoA the intensity from childhood carries over into the workplace and everything is taken *very* seriously.

Adult Children Of Alcoholics Have Difficulty With Intimate Relationships

ACoAs want very much to have healthy intimate relationships, but doing so is extraordinarily difficult for a number of reasons.

The first and most obvious reason is that they have no frame of reference for a healthy intimate relationship because they have not seen one. The only model they have is their parents' relationship, which you and I know was not healthy.

They also carry with them the experience of "come close, go away," a parent-child relationship that is inconsistently loving. They feel loved one day and rejected the next. They grow up with a terrible fear, the fear of being abandoned. If the fear isn't overwhelming, it certainly gets in the way. Not knowing what it is like to have a consistent, day-to-day, healthy intimate relationship with another person makes building one very complicated and painful.

The fear of abandonment gets in the way of developing a relationship. The development of any healthy relationship requires a lot of give and take and problem-solving. There is always some disagreement and anger for a couple to resolve. A minor disagreement gets very big very quickly for adult children of alcoholics because the issue of being abandoned takes precedence over the original issue.

These overwhelming fears of being abandoned or rejected prevent any ease in the process of developing a relationship. These fears are coupled with a sense of urgency — "This is the only time I have; if I don't do it now, it will never happen" — that tends to put pressure on the relationship. This sense of urgency makes it much more difficult to evolve slowly, to let two people get to know each other better and to explore each other's feelings and attitudes in a variety of ways.

This sense of urgency makes the other person feel smothered, even though smothering is not the intent. I know a couple who have tremendous problems because whenever they argue, she panics and worries that he is now going to leave her. She needs constant reassurance in the middle of the argument that he's not going to leave her and that he still loves her. When he is in conflict, which is difficult for him as well, he tends to want to withdraw and be by himself because he is fearful of being aggressive. But if he tries to be alone, she panics even more. If he can't be alone, he feels smothered. Needless to say, this makes the issue at hand more difficult to resolve than if it were only the issue itself needing to be confronted.

The feelings of being insecure, of having difficulty in trusting and questions about whether or not you're going to get hurt are not exclusive to adult children of alcoholics. These are problems most people have. Few people enter a relationship fully confident that things are going to work out the way they hope. They enter a relationship full of hope but with a variety of fears.

The things that cause you concern are not unique to you. It's simply a matter of degree; being a child of an alcoholic caused the ordinary difficulties to become more severe.

What this means in the workplace is that . . .

1. ACoAs have trouble with boundaries, so they don't know how much and what information about themselves to share with fellow workers and supervisors.
2. They will not know how to assess what is a compliment and what is exploitation — be it sexual harassment or a personal favor.

Adult Children Of Alcoholics Over-react To Changes Over Which They Have No Control

As a young child of an alcoholic, you were not in control. The alcoholic's life was inflicted on you, as was your environment. In order to survive when growing up, you needed to begin taking charge of your environment. This became very important and remains so. As a child of an alcoholic you learned to trust yourself more than anyone else when it was impossible to rely on someone else's judgment.

As a result, you are very often accused of being controlling, rigid and lacking in spontaneity. This is probably true. It doesn't come from wanting to do everything your own way. It isn't because you are spoiled or unwilling to listen to other ideas. It comes from the fear that if you are not in charge, if a change is made abruptly, quickly and without your being able to participate in it, you will lose control of your life.

When you look back on your reaction and your behavior later you feel somewhat foolish, but at the time you were simply unable to shift gears.

What this means in the workplace is that for the ACoA . . .

1. Any change involves some loss of one's identity.
2. Adjustment to change involves experiencing the old fears of inadequacy and discovery.

Adult Children Of Alcoholics Constantly Seek Approval And Affirmation

We talk about an external and an internal locus of control. When a child is born, the environment pretty much dictates how he is going to feel about himself. The school, the church and other people all have influence, but the most important influence is what we call "significant others." In the child's world, this usually means his parents. So the child begins to believe who he is by the messages that he gets from his parents. And as he gets older these messages become internalized and contribute significantly to his self-image. The movement is toward the internal locus of control.

The message that you got as a child was very confused. It was not unconditional love. It was not, "I think you're terrific, but I'm not too happy about what you just did." The definitions were not clear and the messages were mixed. "Yes, no, I love you, go away."

So you grew up with some confusion about yourself. The affirmations you didn't get on a day-to-day basis as a child, you interpret as negative.

Now when affirmation is offered, it's very difficult to accept. Accepting the affirmation would be the beginning of changing one's self-image.

What this means in the workplace is that . . .

1. Since ACoAs cannot affirm themselves, they look for affirmation from supervisors and co-workers.
2. They will overwork in order to get strokes.
3. They become convinced that the next promotion will provide personal validation.

Adult Children Of Alcoholics Feel That They Are Different From Other People

ACoAs also assume that in any group of people, everyone else feels comfortable and they are the only ones who feel awkward. This is not peculiar to them. Never, of course, does anyone check it out to find out that each person has his own way of trying not to look awkward. Is that true of you too?

Interestingly enough, you even feel different in a group of adult children of alcoholics. Feeling different is something you have had with you since childhood, and even if the circumstance does not warrant it, the feeling prevails. Other children had an opportunity to be children. You didn't. You were very much concerned with what was going on at home. You could never be completely comfortable playing with other children. You could not be fully there. Your concerns about your home problems clouded everything else in your life.

What happened to you is what happened to the rest of your family. You became isolated. As a result, socializing, being a part of any group, became increasingly difficult. You simply did not develop the social skills necessary to feel comfortable or a part of the group.

It is hard for children of alcoholics to believe that they can be accepted because of who they are and that this acceptance does not have to be earned.

What this means in the workplace is that ACoAs will comply with any requests and demands, regardless of how appropriate or inappropriate they are, because they don't want to be discovered as being different.

Adult Children Of Alcoholics Are Either
Super-Responsible Or Super-Irresponsible

Either you take it all on or you give it all up. There is no middle ground. You tried to please your parents, doing more and more, or you reached the point where you recognized it didn't matter, so you did nothing. You also did not see a family whose members cooperated with each other. You didn't have a family that decided on Sunday, "Let's all work in the yard. I will work on this, and you work on that and then we'll come together."

Not having a sense of being a part of a project, of how to cooperate with other people and let all the parts come together and become a whole, you either do all of it, or you do none of it. You also don't have a good sense of your own limitations. Saying no is extraordinarily difficult for you, so you do more and more and more. You do not do it because you really have a bloated sense of yourself; you do it (1) because you don't have a realistic sense of your capacity or (2) because you are afraid that if you say no, they will find you out. They will find out that you are incompetent. The quality of the job you do does not seem to influence your feelings about yourself. So you take on more and more and more . . . until you finally burn out.

What this means in the workplace is that . . .

1. ACoAs have difficulty sharing responsibility since they have no experience with operating in a cooperative atmosphere; they take it all on or back away entirely.
2. They find it difficult to trust that others will do what they have agreed to do.
3. They may judge the performances of others and the organization in the same merciless way they judge themselves.

Adult Children Of Alcoholics Are Extremely Loyal
Even In The Face Of Evidence That
The Loyalty Is Undeserved

The alcoholic home appears to be a very loyal place. Family members hang in long after reason dictates that they should leave. The so-called loyalty is more the result of fear and insecurity than anything else; nevertheless, the behavior that is modeled is one where no one walks away just because the going gets rough. This sense enables the adult child to remain in involvements that would be better dissolved.

Since making a friend or developing a relationship is so difficult and so complicated, once the effort has been made, it is permanent. If someone cares enough about you to be your friend, your lover or your spouse, then you have the obligation to stay with them forever. If you have let them know who you are, if they have discovered who you are and not rejected you, that fact, in and of itself, is enough to make you sustain the relationship. The fact that they may treat you poorly does not matter. You can rationalize that. Somehow no matter what they do or say, you can figure out a way to excuse their behavior and find yourself at fault. This reinforces your negative self-image and enables you to stay in the relationship. Your loyalty is unparalleled.

What this means in the workplace is that . . .

1. "If they were kind enough to hire me, I owe them my loyalty."
2. The ACoA will give loyalty immediately and automatically.

Adult Children Of Alcoholics Are Impulsive

They tend to lock themselves into a course of action without giving serious consideration to alternative behaviors or possible consequences. This impulsivity leads to confusion, self-loathing and loss of control over their environment. In addition, they spend an excessive amount of energy cleaning up the mess.

As a child you could not predict the outcome of any given behavior, so you don't know how to do it now. Also there was no consistency at home. As a result, you haven't the following framework of "When I behaved impulsively in the past, this happened and that happened and this person reacted in that way." Sometimes it would go okay and sometimes it wouldn't. Essentially, it may not have really mattered. Nor did anyone say to you, "These are the possible consequences of that behavior. Let's talk about other things that you might do."

What this means in the workplace is that . . .

1. ACoAs have difficulty with decision-making, so they will behave impulsively.
2. Since separation issues are so difficult, they will tend to move on quickly rather than deal with them.

2
The Home
Away From Home

Regardless of the nature of their work or the status of their occupation, children of alcoholics have similar feelings about themselves on the job and about their work. In a study of 236 ACoAs, 30 percent of the men and women interviewed reported that they feel inadequate. There is no indication that these feelings have a basis in the rational world.

Feelings of inadequacy and of being unappreciated, of boredom and of perfectionism create stress. That stress comes primarily from using energy to repress these feelings and from keeping others from discovering them. The stress is worsened when ACoAs lack an understanding of how to deal with these feelings in constructive ways.

As a result, issues out of the past get played out in the workplace just as they do everywhere else. It is not unusual for the ACoA to find that his workplace home is a lot like his childhood home.

Duplicating The Family Of Origin

In many ways the workplace is a home away from home. Co-workers become siblings and those in authority take on the role of parent. The work environment is set up like this.

Where the workplace differs from the home is the degree of intimacy one experiences there. Since ACoAs have difficulty with boundaries, they have difficulty maintaining an appropriate and comfortable social and emotional climate with their supervisors and peers. The relationships are unclear because the ACoAs swing between trying to "parent" their superiors and being enabled by their peers.

As a result of this swing, unresolved anger and dependency needs will be played out in their work relationships.

Another dynamic that surfaces is covering up for those who exhibit alcohol and drug problems. ACoAs also enable co-workers by picking up the slack for those who don't do their part. This behavior is encouraged by the system. "We all pitched in" is a fairly common attitude that management likes to foster among its employees.

Once the co-dependency begins, conditions invariably worsen, regardless of the job situation; the ACoA will take on total responsibility — or give it all away. The reality is that once the co-dependency takes over, reason leaves and is replaced by fantasy. This happens very slowly so it is most difficult to realize when it is happening. Eventually anger and fear alternate as the prevailing responses to the work environment, with the occasional plateau where the ACoA believes that everything is fine — until the next time. It is a repeat of childhood.

Ruth is someone I know well. She is a very capable, conscientious professional who is very much aware of her co-dependent responses. I mention that so you can keep in mind that the awareness is only the first step. Without awareness, growth is impossible, but awareness without action is of dubious value.

I am an ACoA and an alcoholism counselor. I am one of ten children. My mother is the alcoholic. She is a periodic binge drinker, the standard Jekyll-and-Hyde alcoholic. When sober, she is beautiful, brilliant, caring and responsible. When drinking, she is ugly, sick and unavailable for a week or two weeks at a time. Father is a textbook co-alcoholic. He is himself the son of two alcoholic parents. He abstains from alcohol. He is a self-made man, the breadwinner of the family, the one who takes over as much as possible when mother is drinking. My brothers and sisters all have at least one of the identified roles adopted by alcoholic children. Growing up, I assumed the roles of mascot, lost child and family hero.

I am 27 years old, three years recovering from my own alcohol and drug dependency, two years in ACoA and Al-Anon, and a year and a half in therapy with a wonderful, very skillful therapist. Severe depression, anxiety and a problematic marriage brought me to therapy. The process of therapy for me was hard and painful. As I moved through the muck, the depression lifted and I gained a perspective on where I came from, how it affected me and what I need to be doing in the present. I began to not feel guilty about taking care of myself. This new perspective changed my behavior, my thinking and my feelings. I finished the necessary course work for certification and my master's degree program. When I separated from my husband, I had no job and no money. But I kept going to meetings and therapy and I got a job.

The agency where I work is an out-patient treatment center. The clientele is primarily alcohol and chemically dependent. The staff is basically trained in chemical dependency. The organizational structure is an executive director, three program supervisors, four full-time therapists and four part-time therapists. The similarities between being one of a staff of 12 and being one of a family of 12 never crossed my mind. I was hired at the same time as two other full-time therapists. Our primary supervisor is Bob. Bob is attractive, witty and well versed in therapeutic interventions. During the first three months of this job, I divorced my husband and developed very intimate relationships with my co-workers. The work schedule was extremely difficult. I worked mostly in the evenings and I was expected to carry 25 individual clients, as well as families and groups, in a 40-hour work week. It is a community agency, so no one is turned away.

I was feeling good about myself as an individual and with what I was doing with my clients and co-workers. During this period I was not alone in wondering what was happening in my life. The other therapists were also working to get acclimatized and settled.

Relatively early on, I started asking questions, sometimes getting answers to my questions, sometimes not. My supervisor would tell me he would get back to me and would forget or not attend to the question asked.

The staff brought new skills, new ambitions and new energy into this agency. We presented our ideas, thoughts and feelings on new programs, new groups and new treatment to the supervisor and to the administrator. They'd agree, they'd acknowledge that all of these ideas and programs were needed and necessary. They encouraged us to go on.

When we asked for what we needed to carry out this work, they would tell us that they would get back to us and didn't. The months continued and the frustration grew. We began to notice that the supervisors would play ball with responsibility. They would toss responsibility from one to the other, back to the administrator, back down to the supervisors and come back to the staff with nothing — no concrete answers to the questions, no materials or support for the therapists to do their jobs. When I got in touch with my frustration, I initially would try to use one of my three programs by reminding myself during these moments to *let go and let God.* I found out that I could no longer *let go and let God* when there wasn't a chair for the client or somebody to answer the phones that were constantly ringing.

All of the line staff identified feelings of abandonment, anger and frustration. As a group we supported each other and helped each other to get through the moment. As individuals we would go back to the supervisor and ask again for what we needed. Sixty percent of the time we didn't get what we needed, 20 percent of the time he wouldn't be there to ask and 20 percent of the time we got what we needed.

I tried to respect the supervisor and his authority, until I realized that he was not worthy of my respect. The staff then consulted with the administrator on the problems we had in dealing with the supervisor. She would console us and tell us it was wrong and that she would do something about it.

She would then meet individually with the supervisor and let him know that she expected a change. There would be a brief period of change and then the supervisor would relapse to his old behavior, irresponsible and unpredictable.

As this pattern continued, the frustration began to feel familiar. I knew it from somewhere else as well. At a staff meeting one day I sat at the end of the table and looked at the faces. I looked at the administrator and I looked at the supervisors. There were 12 people there. I knew that what I was reacting to was my family of origin. My supervisor was my alcoholic mother. The administrator who consoled and worked hard and wished that things would change was my father.

Several of the other staff, the quiet ones, were the lost children. There were also mascots and family heroes on the staff.

I had developed a new role here that I never had in my own family. I was a scapegoat. The supervisors felt that I was stirring up trouble. If it weren't for my complaints and my demands, everyone would feel better on the job. There were statements being made during the staff meeting but I couldn't hear them. I kept looking around the table. I identified which staff person behaved like one of my brothers or sisters. I clearly saw what I was reacting to and it made me more angry. I was enraged that a treatment facility working with sick individuals and families could let this happen.

When I gained this insight into my anger, I experienced hope, hope that now that I knew what was going on, now that the problem was identified, changes could be made.

I met with the administrator and shared my thoughts with her. Ironically she is the ex-wife of an alcoholic. I told her that I thought she was enabling the supervisor by allowing him to continue his destructive behavior patterns. Again I let her know that his behavior was affecting me and other staff members. She turned to another supervisor who was more responsible to clean up the mess. That worked for a week. My resentment continued to grow.

The administrator created problems because she didn't want to hurt anyone. Her answer to the problem of Bob was to change his position from supervisor to public relations.

I never saw Bob do his job as a public relations person either. I was relieved with this insight. I could see so clearly what I was reacting to. Once I saw that there would be no change, I felt empowered. I had to leave to take care of myself. This I did. I had left home once and I could do it again. At least this time, having done my best, I recognized my powerlessness and knew I had to move on.

Another example of an alcoholic family system involved Jean. Jean is a keypunch operator and has been for 20 years. Her company is installing a new machine and she is terrified that she will be unable to learn the system and will lose her job. She gets paralyzed at the training sessions.

The person in charge of the training explains things quickly and leaves out important information. Those who know her say she does this because she is frightened that if others get too good, she will lose her authority.

When someone asks a question, she makes the person wait for the answer while she does makeshift work. The trainee is sitting in the office doing nothing while everyone else is busy. The trainee feels awkward and awful and becomes certain they are all aware of the fact that she is stupid. When the question is finally answered, it's answered in such a way as to imply that anyone with half a brain would have understood the first time.

A typical response to this behavior would be anger, not paralysis. It therefore becomes important to discover what the paralysis means.

When growing up, Jean was always told by her alcoholic father how stupid she was, and she believed him. She was also told to do things around the house but never told how and then got yelled at if she asked. She would then be beaten if she didn't do it right. She knew it had to do with her because she didn't think the same thing happened to her twin sister. She found out later that it did happen to her sister, but her sister suffered more silently.

It is no surprise that Jean would become frozen when placed in a situation that is so much like her childhood. It is a replay of the same scene.

The difference here is that with this insight, Jean no longer has to be the victim and can take action to ensure that she will be treated in a more respectful manner.

Co-dependency in its simplest terms is a loss of personal power. It is characterized by giving over control of one's ego to another.

If co-dependency is loosely defined as the giving away of personal power, the answers lie in how to be personally powerful and maintain that power; how to be active and not reactive; how to take appropriate responsibility but not allow others to induce guilt.

In the first case the answer lay in leaving the job; in the second case, the answer lay in being more confrontational.

Functioning within the first system became impossible. In the second, when the training is complete the contact with the person who precipitates the co-dependent response is also over.

The context in which the bad feelings emerge is relevant to the resolution.

3
The ACoA

One of my assumptions when I began researching this book was that children of alcoholics are found predominantly in stressful occupations. But it became apparent to me that ACoAs are represented in all job categories. The occupational choices seemed to follow those of the general population. In a survey of 238 people, eight were clerical workers and eight were managers; four were lawyers and four were bus drivers.

The accounts you will read here demonstrate that, regardless of occupational choice, the qualities inherent in being an ACoA predominate. It appears that stress is created by the ACoA, even when it is not inherent in the job description. The ACoA teacher, technician, religious worker, foreman, airline employee, administrator, nurse, athlete, soldier or officer, waitress and medical student all have much in common.

The ACoA Teacher

Since I see myself as typical of ACoAs who have entered the teaching profession, the best way for me to describe "them" is to let you know me.

It is only in the past five years or so that I have realized the impact of my parents' alcoholism on my life and how I have led that life, including decisions that I have made. Both of my parents are active alcoholics and probably have been for at least the last 30 of my 42 years.

The only career aspiration I ever had was to be a teacher. I programmed myself to like school before I ever entered. My efforts to do well and to gain recognition paid off in terms of teacher acceptance and personal achievement that continued throughout my academic career. By my own choice I attended Catholic schools from first grade through college . . . 16 years. I was elected to the National Honor Society, graduated *magna cum laude* from college and always received exemplary grades in conduct.

Making my parents proud was my expressed reason for my need to excel, although I was deeply shamed by the occasional lower grade and/or teacher dissatisfaction. I often made deals with God (and with St. Joseph Cupertino, patron saint of test-takers) for inspiration to do well with papers and reports and on tests. Having achieved success, I was convinced that my decision to be a teacher was a good one.

I liked the sense of control I had in the classroom. I was in charge! I made the rules and, most important, people did what I wanted them to do. A big fish in a little pond, I believed that my life would have the order and purpose that I was unable to make happen at home with my parents.

And such a teacher! I prepared with zeal — not content to have one source, I researched many, to leave out nothing. I wonder now if those early lessons made much sense to those 4th graders, chock-full as they were with all of that researched information. This need to be a Super Teacher points out the other side of that control issue: my personal feeling of lack of control accompanied by my fear of exposing the fear and inadequacy I was experiencing.

I felt an urgent need for my classroom to be a place where youngsters felt safe and appreciated. No "What the hell happened with Science, you only got an A-" in my class! I worked very hard to reach every youngster, feeling guilty when I thought about those youngsters who remained shy or ignorant of a subject/chapter/lesson in spite of my hardest efforts to inspire and to educate. Actually, I was angry with them for not coming along. I was frustrated with my lack of success with them. I was hurt that they did not like me. It never occurred to me then that those children and I might have something in common — a dysfunctional, if not alcoholic, family.

When, equipped with my fear of close relationships and my unfamiliarity with emotional intimacy, I reached out to those youngsters, I was asking of those children what I was unwilling to share: feelings, fears, worries, "secrets." I was very sensitive to what I perceived as their rejection of me.

I also appreciated the isolation of the classroom. There I could attempt to be all things to each student without a peer audience. In addition, I prided myself on never asking anyone for help. "I am capable" was my facade. Only I knew the scared little girl behind it.

To pretend that all was not only well but excellent, and certainly under control, I decided — the first year that I taught — to have my 4th grade present a play during the day for the other students and in the evening for parents. (At the time, I was several months pregnant with my first child and determined that none of this would affect the Super Wife I presented to my husband.) Not content to settle for anything pre-packaged, I wrote the play . . . and the songs (after a self-taught crash course in piano-playing) . . . and planned and executed the elaborate scenery and costumes (it involved the illusion of descending beneath the ocean and finding an underwater kingdom) . . .

One day as my class was working on various tasks related to the play (painting, drawing, sewing, singing, rehearsing), the principal entered the room. Walking to a cabinet on her sweep of the room, she came to me and informed me that there was dust on the cabinet. I had managed to find a principal with my father's ability to remind me that I would never be good enough. Fascinating how the fear of being found out was tied in with the need to prove myself, which led to my overextension. Incidentally, the play was a great success but I can only truly appreciate and remember it as such within the recent past.

Ultimately I decided to return to college for a Master's degree in Counseling, again with a dedication to achieving As. When I got that degree, I became a junior high school guidance counselor. I made it a point to understand the master schedule and its planning; I reminded the Director of Guidance of deadlines; I excelled at the efficient expedition of necessary paperwork, which was not the forte of the two men with whom I counseled, so I often did all the paperwork myself and usually at home so that my time with students would not be impeded. Throughout this period, I was striving to enhance the image of the Guidance Department and to fulfill my prime purpose of being available and helpful to students and concomitantly to parents and staff. This meant no coffee breaks except at my desk while working. It meant no regular lunch times or departure times. This began to change five years ago when I faced up to my problems as the adult child of an alcoholic and began to really live my own life.

The ACoA Manager

A manager of the Employee Assistance Program at a high-tech research firm has this to say about ACoAs on the job:

The composite profile I have observed is that of an individual with good credentials who is very capable, who, however, lacks self-confidence. ACoAs have used the high-technology environment to avoid dealing with people. They see themselves as different, on the outside looking in, and not really part of the group. They often become so isolated that they can no longer communicate in other than technical terms.

ACoAs do not expect anything from relationships beyond technical support and they don't get anything. Their isolation grows until they find themselves in a situation in which they can no longer function. They reduce all human tasks to analytical terms, seen through technical paradigms. The smallest task becomes a major technical issue. Because the interpersonal world is not always logical in technical terms, they feel more and more like failures, using human fallibility as evidence for their lack of self-worth.

By the time these people come to me, they actually do look different. They often dress very plainly, are poorly groomed and seem to have simply dropped out of the social mainstream. These folks are wonderful employees as long as they do not have to interact socially or get involved with what they see as "political games." A serious problem is that sometimes they are promoted and they make awful supervisors.

As supervisors, they are demanding and sometimes unrealistic but they don't delegate authority. They do not trust their subordinates and ask to have every assignment repeated over and over. Sometimes they seem very pleased and the next moment they are screaming at the subordinate in public. Later they may return tearful and apologetic. They can't be pleased.

Some indicate that they feel like frauds and know that they will be fired if the company finds out what they are really like, even if they are actually very competent. Their victims are their subordinates who come to the Employee Assistance Program feeling abused, terribly confused and often ready to give up.

The ACoA Medical Student

Professional schools have always been very stressful places but they are particularly stressful for ACoAs. The system is designed to teach humility and confidence, to make students work to the limits of their endurance — just what the ACoA doctor ordered, as Tom tells us of his experience in medical school:

In the dysfunctional family I grew up in, we were expected to do two things perfectly — schoolwork and being nice to other people. *Perfectly* meant straight As, always having adults compliment your behavior and doing this all apparently without effort and without mistakes.

I was "perfect" up through college when I just had to learn and take tests and no one had to know me. But medical school was different; I went into medical school thinking I'd be a hero who would do something wonderful for people that no one else had ever done. It seems silly but what else could I do? I'd been taught to get my self-esteem from being better/smarter than everyone else and by making myself liked by everyone.

The first two years were more books and tests — only now there was more work than I could do perfectly. Besides, medical school is full of people who'd been top students and I was no longer effortlessly best in my class. I got average scores and tried to tell myself I could have been tops if I'd worked at it but that never satisfied me. No longer being the smartest punctured my self-image.

Medical school is training for novices and, in truth, we have to learn from our mistakes and from seeing that we need to learn more. But if an attending physician pointed out a mistake

I'd made, or something I didn't know (but should have), or just didn't seem interested in me, I felt imperfect, bad and at fault. I didn't want people to see that.

Unfortunately medicine is traditionally taught by taking a top student, giving him more to learn than he can, giving him no priorities as to what to learn — "Everything is important; I wouldn't expect you to learn it if it weren't" — and then ridiculing and demeaning him and telling him he's useless until he thinks he got into medical school by mistake.

My perfectionism, people-pleasing and readiness to accept blame made me an ideal set-up for this system. Throughout most of my medical training I felt guilty about becoming a doctor. I thought I didn't want it enough to deserve it, that I'd never learn enough to be competent. At the same time I was expected to exude confidence and authority with patients.

The next two years I had to deal with individuals — the doctors (attendings) who were my teachers — and my patients. In retrospect, I see that these people were not out to make me miserable but what I'd learned in my family made these close relationships painful. Growing up I'd been told I was smart and kind. These were the positive attributes I identified with and I needed to keep hearing them.

Attendings rarely had time to teach, needed us to do some of their work, and trusted us to do things if only they thought we already knew how. The only way for us to get experience was to pretend we already had it. This didn't fit with my idea of perfect patient care but I did it, got the experience I needed and felt guilty and phony.

On the other hand, my patients liked me, listened to me, wanted to see me and told me I was important to them. I was taught that I should look at patients clinically but I didn't. I needed some positive strokes. This led to even longer hours as I spent more time with patients. I felt guilty when I went home because I always felt that there was some patient's need I'd left unattended. I had been taught this, as well, by attending staff who often sacrificed their personal lives to their patients. And I found myself becoming at ease with the role of caretaker but not enjoying the rest of my life. Since my personal relationships and free time had never been fun or satisfying, it was easy for me to become a workaholic, even though I started to hate medicine.

The ACoA Priest

The workplace is not exclusively the office, the store or the factory. It can also be the religious community, where the ACoA experiences the same problems that occur anywhere else on the job — and then some!

A counselor who deals with religious communities writes:

> The ACoA in the religious workplace has all the traits of the typical ACoA but there are some added complications. Certain elements in the training of priests, religious sisters and religious brothers seem to be harmful to the ACoA unless they are honestly faced. For instance, religious training frequently has given statements such as . . .
>
> • You are called to be a person for others.
> • You must be all things to all people.
> • Service to others is its own reward.
> • The needs of the community must be addressed before personal needs.
> • You must strive to be perfect.

The religious ACoA has little or no understanding of the need for personal boundaries within the ministry. There is a real difference between religious life and the life of a person who has a secular occupation. When you have an occupation, you can try to separate your work life from your personal life. The religious is unable to do this. Thus it is more difficult to understand the place of boundaries and clearly defined limits in one's work.

The religious ACoA is given strong religious motivation to put others first. Scriptural statements like, "The Son of Man has not come to be served, but to serve and to give his life as a ransom for many," are frequently applied in ways that are harmful rather than helpful. ACoAs in general put others first and themselves last but the religious ACoA is given a powerful theological motivation to do this as well. So when the religious ACoA goes into therapy, there can be tremendous resistance to placing himself first. It is perceived as not simply a matter of personal well-being. It is seen as a direct contradiction of the message that the religious ACoA is supposed to be following.

There are several different reactions that the religious ACoA may have to criticism. One reaction is simply that the religious

ACoA is a bad person. However, another reaction is directly related to the religious calling. If you are criticized for what you do in your ministry, you are not only letting down another person, you are letting down God. Thus, rather than realizing that we often can and do make mistakes, we come to question the whole foundation of our religious commitment.

Statements like these come into the mind of the religious ACoA:

"If I have done this, then I must not be a good priest."
"I am a fraud in my religious vocation."
"I help no one."
"People can see through me."

ACoAs can feel that they are frauds as people. The religious ACoAs believe they are frauds as people and as the type of person they believe God has called them to be.

Loneliness is a particularly acute phenomenon for the religious ACoA. While the idea of living within a religious community theoretically means that sharing can take place, this is often the last place where the religious ACoA can share. When others appear to be striving for perfection, the religious ACoA may feel that he or she is really trying to admit imperfection. This builds up the isolation and creates yet another complication for the religious ACoA.

Intimacy and sexuality are different issues for the religious ACoA who is celibate. The reason religious are celibate is that celibacy enables them to be loving and open with all and to truly serve all in the community. The negative side of this for religious ACoAs is that they need to share their deepest feelings and thoughts. They need to share their past experiences and admit their present inadequacies. But sometimes the religious life may not foster this type of experience, so the sense of loneliness and isolation increases, the ability to be intimate and loving decreases. Obviously, people who are married or in relationships frequently are unable to be intimate and loving. But it seems that the nature of religious life provides a greater sense of loneliness and isolation than other vocations.

The ACoA Foreman

As children, we were often told, "Work very hard and you'll be rewarded." Companies sometimes support and reinforce this message. Hank is a case in point — a guy who worked so hard that he almost lost his job.

I've worked for a public utility for about 14 years now, and of those 14 years, I spent approximately 12 at a power plant. I began with the company as a laborer, working very hard, long hours outside in the field. Then I went "inside" to the power plant.

I was always taught that if you work very hard, you'll be rewarded by a job, so to speak, or a promotion. I've now found out that it's a little different. When I went into the power plant, I began as a stockman. What I did in this position was off-load trucks, along with various kinds of paperwork, until I moved up into my position as a material clerk, which consisted of controlling 40,000 or so spare parts.

My job was to see that each part was classified and broken down into sub-systems and defined as either mechanical, electrical or instrumentation parts; then to assign each part a particular six-digit catalogue number which referenced that part to the part number and established a minimum/maximum for the part; then to find it and store it in one of eight warehouses. There was also a ledger system and an index so that when employees came in, they would be able to locate the part they wanted. This manual system was also transferred into a computer. I worked very hard and very long (ten hours a day, seven days a week). In fact, I averaged 550 to 575 hours of overtime per year. My travel time to and from work was an hour's drive, so I would get up at 5:30 each morning to go to work and would leave work about 5:45 to go home.

This still wasn't enough work for me. I spent four and a half years building a house and I would sometimes stay up until 3:00 a.m., sleep on my way to work (I car pooled), sleep on my lunch hours, catch another couple of hours of sleep after work, then get up around 9:00 p.m. and work most of the night on the house. I was always taught that if you want something, you have to work for it.

I went through a marriage; I just came out of a relationship; and I find at age 35 that I really don't know who the hell I am! Everybody looks at me and idolizes me because I can do everything.

Like I said, I built that house — designed it, framed it, did all the plumbing, the electrical work, insulated it, dry-walled it, spackled it, sanded it, wallpapered it, did the outside stone work (with the help of some friends), etc. The house is approximately 3,500 square feet, it has 13 rooms and I'm the only one living there! This sounds funny but it's true. I found out that my life-long dream was actually more like my coffin. On my job I never refused overtime. In fact, for nine of those eleven and a half years on my company rating report, I was described as a very loyal employee, never refusing overtime and always willing and available for work. I thought that was good. You work for a company, you're a responsible individual. It was part of your job assignment to be responsible when something happened in that particular operation — which ran 24 hours a day, seven days a week, holidays included. I worked many Easters, Thanksgivings, and double shifts. I would go home, be called back out and off I'd go again. I had it good there. It paid well and I had many good benefits. I had a stove at work, a crockpot and a blender; but I found out that when my job was done (11 other people left that job because it was "crazy" or "not worth it"), I was the only one who had stuck it out because I had confidence in my ability.

But this got me into a lot of trouble. It caused my divorce because I would never say no to overtime. I got into many arguments with my immediate supervisor because I carried things too far at times in trying to be perfect.

I was always too serious. People always tell me I'm too serious — I never laughed. It got to the point where I wouldn't even socialize with my friends because I felt my job was more important. I wanted to get ahead so I worked very hard for this. I even went to school for three years to get a Purchasing degree. I joined the Purchasing Management Association (none of the company buyers, other than the head buyer, belonged to this association), and this cost me money for which I wasn't even reimbursed. I even took personal vacation time to attend a seminar so I could get one point toward my certification at the university.

I felt this was good. I was gearing myself towards a better position. I attended a meeting of the PMA every week and made a point of having lunch with one of the buyers to discuss work. When the job was done, though, the system was functioning and I was bored!

When I got bored, I got into trouble. I was picked to join the Activities Committee, the Safety and Health Committee, Plant

Betterment Committee, Fire Protection Committee. I belonged to all of these! I started running company bus trips, at first once a month, then once every weekend, then twice and even three times every weekend. People were calling me at work constantly and this caused problems with my immediate supervisor and his supervisor. They thought I wasn't doing my job because they considered this a sideline, even though it was company-oriented. I was told I would only be given an hour per week for these activities. But I kept on doing it until I was reprimanded and told to either stop or be removed from the committee. At the time I was VP of the committee for approximately 1,000 people. When I took over the position, the "kitty" was almost in the red, but at the end of the year we were $1,000.00 in the black.

I was doing a good job in that respect. I was neglecting my duties on my full-time job but the job was done and everything was running smoothly. Even so, this was a problem for the company because I didn't *seem* to be there. My supervisor was very upset over having to answer my phone all the time. I finally decided to take a voluntary demotion and I left that installation to be closer to corporate headquarters.

My voluntary demotion was a mistake. I lost $153.00 a week and went from a B-8 status down to a B-2, just so I could be closer to the corporate office, figuring they would recognize that I have so much experience under my belt, my certifications, membership in the PMA, etc. I had bid on several jobs and was turned down for various reasons.

My former boss of nine years retired and I put in for his position. I didn't hear anything for approximately two months and then I got a letter. I didn't even open it right away because I was so confident of getting an interview for the position. I even went out and bought a new suit, new shoes, etc., for the big interview. Well, lo and behold, when I opened the letter I found that, out of 30 applicants, I was placed on a level where I wouldn't even be considered for an interview.

This was the reason I went to see the counselor and she said I looked like somebody had taken a knife and cut me in half. I felt, boy oh boy, I had put all my eggs in one basket and look what happened!

Of course, I was told not to be discouraged because something would eventually come my way and I believe it will. The day I got that rejection letter, I walked and walked and walked for at least five miles on my lunch hour, and I wasn't even going to return to work. I was going to say "BS" to the company. But the bottom line is that the company really doesn't owe me anything other than 40 hours' pay for 40 hours' work. I guess I'm obsessed with being a perfectionist and thinking that if you work hard for a company, you go down with the company — like the captain of a sinking ship.

The ACoA Airline Employee

Another EAP counselor, working this time in the airline industry, says this about his ACoA workers:

ACoAs who come to me for help often have a very strong work history and are often self- and supervisor-described as very conscientious. For those whose job performance was deficit and who were referred by supervisors, I noticed that I was able to trace a historical point when excellent performance was interrupted by a progressive decline. ACoAs often report that their performance on the job and the company are very important to them.

The advent of deregulation has resulted in a change from a nurturing paternalistic management style to one that is demanding and results-oriented, and a more pressured work environment. Some ACoAs adjust well to these changes and appear to identify with the needed company changes as a survival need. Some experience an anxiety and pain related to being unable to please passengers and respond to their demands or not being affirmed by supervisors, as in the past.

ACoAs appear more likely to assume a special caretaking relationship with troubled employees. This is reflected in supervisors and co-workers who invest energy in helping and taking responsibility for the maintenance of their jobs. They have often sought help in the past that did not address their needs.

It appears that many of their problems are related to interpersonal difficulties which often escalate and cause a great deal of anxiety. This is often connected with family difficulties that have become unmanageable. Often the loss and abandonment themes seem to be connected with this issue and result in either job deterioration or a great deal of energy expended on the job to no effect.

The ACoA Administrator

Bureaucracy often provides the firm guidelines children of alcoholics need to have — where they stand in relation to their fellow employees, what they are supposed to do — but these boundaries can often mean nothing to a hardworking ACoA. ACoAs have the ability to turn a part-time job into a full-time occupation, as Bill shows here in his account of the work he did to support his graduate studies.

I was involved in the dormitory administration of a big university on the west coast, first as a front desk staffer, later as a front desk supervisor and finally as an acting front desk manager. I achieved this in the space of only three years, during which I also worked full-time on my graduate studies, participated in residence halls' politics and worked on behalf of the students in my department on the Graduate Fine Arts Council. Somewhere in there, I was also trying to conduct a "meaningful" relationship with a fellow student.

From the start, I was very hard-working and conscientious. In part, it was out of gratitude for having a job where I lived — just a hallway away. And it had come at a time when I was still waiting for my student loan and had no money at all, so I also felt indebted to the people who hired me. I worked all kinds of shifts — daytime and late-night. I did all kinds of special jobs and projects that demanded a great deal of attention to detail and I know that I did them well. I was pleasant to work with, pleasant to the hall residents and the rest of the staff. I was popular and eager to solve problems.

After being on the staff for a year and a half, working both the Christmas and summer breaks, I was offered the supervisor position. Despite the fact that I was in the middle of preparing for my comprehensive exams, I took on the job.

From the start as supervisor, I began to do more and more at the front desk. It wasn't just a matter of the added responsibilities of the job; it was a matter of picking up on everything that was happening there. Nothing could happen without my supervision, without my approval. I was on call 24 hours a day, and I had a real sense of anxiety every time I left the building. One time, I jokingly told a friend that as the dorm sank into sea, I would be standing at attention on the bridge. Some joke!

I began to feel that I was overextending myself, so I dropped the residence hall and campus politics over the summer. But then I had too much time on my hands — too much for the front desk, although I was working about 30 hours a week; too much for my papers and academic work, although that was taking up another 40 or 50 hours; too much for trying to make the relationship work. As a result, I took on a research assistantship to fill in the quiet hours.

As supervisor I took tremendously good care of my staff. Since I was taking several independent study courses, I spent less time in the classroom, so when one of the staff had an exam to prepare for, I would take over her shift. When a resident was having a problem with a roommate, I would talk with him about it and help him to resolve it.

The one thing I did not play by the book when I was supervisor was the huge amount of paperwork. It was my conviction that the purpose of bureaucracy of that sort was to lay blame, and I wanted my staff to know and feel that I had trust and confidence in them, even though I was spending so much time down at the front desk that trust wasn't really an issue — I would always be there for them, quite literally.

The manager retired after I had finally passed my exams and since I knew the job so well, I thought I was the logical successor. But the university was in the midst of a hiring freeze, and all I could do was assume the role of the manager but not the title or the pay. I felt, in a sense, that I had to take on the added responsibilities because the general manager of the dorm was new on the job and didn't know how it worked. I was told, in any case, that a special exemption might be made for our dorm and that I would get the position very soon.

The *soon* was first two months, then three. I spoke vaguely to my boss about getting some kind of pay raise, but pay scales had been frozen in the freeze, too. I asked him about filing for the exemption and he said that he "would look into it." I began to get a little restless as three months dragged into six.

Then I decided to take action. I wrote to the University Ombudsman, the Residence Halls Administrator and the Dean responsible for university housing. I said nothing about any of this to my boss but I was getting tired of working at the front desk, tired of the hassles with my girlfriend and generally tired of the university. I started to smoke a lot of dope and work on my music. I took no classes at all in my final term and worked at the desk only during the days. I was waiting for something — anything — to happen.

And things did happen in quick succession. The first was that the Ombudsman's office had called my boss, not me, and I was brought into his office.

"How could you do this to me?"

I responded that I felt I had no choice, that he wasn't doing anything for me.

He replied that he had assumed responsibility for the work I was doing and that I was making him look bad. I apologized, then turned around and fired off a memo to the Residence Halls Administrator saying that I was still doing all this work and enclosed the job descriptions of the front desk supervisor and the front desk manager.

Nothing more happened after that, although I did have another unproductive meeting with my boss. A week later, my girlfriend, supposedly in the middle of summer classes, asked me to put something in her room during the day. I went in that morning and found her in bed with someone else. I couldn't believe it and even now I wonder if it wasn't some kind of hallucination. Whatever the case, I immediately went down to the desk and wrote up my resignation. I finally had the excuse I needed to get away.

The ACoA Nurse

Children of alcoholics very often find themselves in human service occupations, as this nursing supervisor describes:

Nurses are very proud of the fact that they are caretakers; they tend to the suffering and deal with death on a regular basis. As a nurse, I felt good to assist in relieving another's pain. With this in mind, the sense of responsibility that I carried in the name of my patients was overwhelming. I shouldered this responsibility to the point of believing I could hold back death itself.

The small successes and experience of another's joy in the painstaking process of recovery encouraged me to want more. These experiences, combined with the expectations that others had of me, compelled me to demand more of myself. I thought nothing of trying to fill simultaneously the roles of counselor, healer, wife, mother, technician, manager, transporter and M.D. assistant. Denial is evident: I was far removed from the impossibility of what I expected of myself. Guilt is a wonderful motivator for nurses. Viewed by others as an angel of mercy and self-sacrificing, I learned that saying no was just not an acceptable way for me to deal with my limitations. Consequently, I became a skilled manipulator, deal maker and controller of my environment. If these methods didn't work, my temper flared up: martyrdom and excuse-making would.

Generally, an ACoA nurse will readily give up her own instincts and thoughts about her work, a patient or a situation in the presence of an M.D. This surrender by the nurse occurs less frequently with supervisors but nonetheless it does happen. These people were intimidating to me, for they represented authority. They were all-knowing and had power.

Among my peers, I occasionally released my emotions — most often in the form of anger. Wittiness and humor also worked well to relieve my load. Resentment, self-pity and resignation weighed me down. When asked about my feelings I quickly deflected the question, gave excuses or flatly denied their existence. Clearly I was uncomfortable, quite possibly because I was out of touch with my feelings. I met thoughts of changing my situation or expanding my abilities with an air of sadness. As an ACoA I offered excuses or simply resigned myself to my plight.

It is not surprising that the ACoA nurse takes pride in creating calm out of chaotic situations. I was a true artist, a magician in seeming to perform the impossible. I returned each day to meet the challenge, for I knew it well; it was a place that felt like home.

The ACoA Waitress

Ever see a waitress carry five plates (four on one arm and a plate in the other hand), take orders on the way to the table for two cups of coffee and a glass of water and still give the right food to the right customer, all from memory? That may be enough for most people to handle, but with an ACoA on the job there's always something more to be done.

When I was 13, I worked as a waitress for a man who owned a pizzeria. Much of the time we were in the restaurant alone.

His business was a bomb, from the food to the wallpaper; he was a very unhappy man. I wanted to make his business an overnight success and solve all his personal problems. I shared my ideas with him and began to make arrangements to help him remodel. I thought that if I could help his business flourish then his personal problems would be solved too. I cared so much that he tried to bang me in the kitchen. My mother found out about this through a careless slip of my tongue and promptly called him on it, scaring the man to tears. He called me, crying and apologizing. Had my mother not intervened, I would've gone back to work, although I was scared out of my mind. Confronting my boss was more terrifying to me than going back.

When I was 16, I worked in a "fine dining" restaurant that was also a bomb. I remained there loyally for about eight months although I was being exploited in several ways. At times I did the work of a manager and cashier at waitress wages ($1.35 per hour) just to "keep busy." My employer once charged me over $100 for cashiering mistakes on credit cards, in spite of the fact that it wasn't my job to handle money and that no one had ever trained me. Naturally, I paid him and reprimanded myself for making the mistakes. My employment there ended after a few such incidents when the Board of Labor and Department of Health became involved.

Most of my restaurant jobs have had similarly dramatic endings. I tend to get so emotionally involved in my work that there is no separation between my job and my personal life. In the beginning my employers like me because I compulsively overwork. Then I begin to get resentful and emotional because no one is considering my feelings and I usually get fired shortly thereafter.

At present I waitress at a restaurant that is very poorly managed. When I first started working there, I worked much harder than humanly possible. If I was the only waitress on and the dining room was jammed, I panicked about trying to take care of all 1,000,000 customers. The thought never entered my mind that maybe they should hire an additional waitress.

The ACoA Athlete

Nobody knows better than an ACoA how to turn play into work. Because ACoAs have difficulty in simply having fun, the games others enjoy in childhood become much more serious. Mark describes his experience and the experience typical of ACoAs who have made a career of something that others do for fun, whether it's in sports or some other field. While other people dream of having a career they can enjoy, an ACoA, in following such a career, puts a lot of effort into making sure he gets no joy out of it at all.

The ACoA Super-Achiever-Athlete (ACoA-SAA) will sacrifice many childhood activities in order to excel in athletics. He may pass up playing with his friends in order to spend time practicing. He may also give up soft drinks, sweets and more, in order to perfect his body.

The ACoA-SAA goes to school to compete and succeed in sports and bring worth to his family and himself. College and pro scouts don't recruit players from the local Boys Club or YMCA, so school is an important institution in which to participate. He studies enough to maintain his 2.5 GPA and continue competing for the school. (If his grades are higher, it is a bonus.)

Like other children of alcoholics, he also spends a great amount of time daydreaming. He will be daydreaming about the winning basket, touchdown or home run, just as his teacher asks him a question. It is important to him to see himself as a winner because he has to battle constantly with an inner voice that tells him he is worthless, unlovable and a failure.

The ACoA-SAA is loyal to his school and coaches. No one wears the school colors louder or prouder. He brings prestige to the school via the media and community acknowledgment. He is usually the team captain and demands the respect of his peers. He sometimes thinks of himself as a player/coach. He will push himself and his teammates to their physical limits in order to prepare for competition.

Some people may say, "It's not whether you win or lose, but how you play the game," but this is blasphemy to the ACoA-SAA. He lives for game nights. He lives to *win, win, win,* because games are his only opportunity to gain recognition and self-respect. If his team wins, he cannot sleep that night because he cannot stop wondering what good things the newspaper will say the following morning. His sense of self-worth depends solely on reported statistics and the printed article.

But the ACoA-SAA is not an impenetrable fortress in the heat of competition; he is actually the most likely to crack under the stress of a game because of the inner voice of failure. There is nothing more awful for him than to hear that voice while attempting to shoot the winning free throw, toss the winning pitch, catch the winning pass or sprint the winning lap. The voice speaks inconsistently but always in the key moment of the competition. When he hears it, his concentration breaks and he makes crucial mistakes.

He interprets losing a game as his individual responsibility and not the team's. The inner voice of failure echoes loudly in his mind, "You are a failure. You blew it again!" He has brief suicidal thoughts. He thinks there is nothing to live for since he has failed everyone who depends on him. He might put his thoughts into action because his self-worth, which was strictly rooted in athletic success, has been shattered. However, he will not display his depression outwardly because he must maintain his stable public image to please others.

He does not compete well at home in front of everyone he knows because he is trying too hard to please the crowd and is rarely relaxed. If he goes away to college and returns to compete against a local school, he will not play well; the inner voice is too loud.

Because he is a people-pleaser, he will allow his peers at school to control his life in the hallways and classrooms. He would rather be alone, though, because he knows he is really a loser.

The ACoA-SAA is most prone to injuries during stressful periods of the season. Consciously, he prepares himself to be in the best physical shape possible for the season, especially for the very important games. Subconsciously, his mind (if under a great deal of internal/external stress) may cause his body to be susceptible to injury. The injury will occur prior to or in the middle of the competition. It will give him a safe excuse not to face the inner voice of failure. Therefore he won't have to take the chance of losing and blaming himself once again. No one else could possibly blame him for the team's loss if he was physically incapable of competing.

The ACoA-SAA's choice of which college to attend is also affected by the inner voice of failure. Though he has the ability to compete at a large university, he will more likely select a smaller school. It is much safer to be a big fish in a small pond.

However, this does not guarantee success at the collegiate level. Only if he can continue to fight the voice and if he gets enough exposure, might he make it to the professional level of competition.

The voice follows the ACoA-SAA into the professional arena, bringing the same emotional havoc he's always known. The inner voice will affect his contract negotiations, his ability to compete and his emotional stability. This is when he is most likely to use alcohol and drugs on a steady basis.

The ACoA In The Military

Not all jobs present the ACoA with boundary problems. Sometimes, as Alan says in his description of military life, they can provide the ACoA with all the rules he needs to get by.

As an adult child of an alcoholic, where better could I find approval and affirmation than in the military? I received instant and lasting recognition for my accomplishments. I spent 20 years in the Navy, the first 12 as a practicing alcoholic, the remainder in recovery. The military offered the perfect atmosphere for this rule-bound ACoA. The system encourages workaholism, unquestioning loyalty, super-responsibility and no questioning or doubt of superiors. The system is rigid and demanding. It dictates what normal is . . . I was home.

My uniform set me apart and it achieved instant status. I wore many of my accomplishments on my chest — awards and ribbons ranging from combat action and achievement to foreign decorations. My gold wings further enhanced my position. On my collar and sleeve you could see my status in the hierarchy and my length of service. In the Navy after 12 years of good conduct (what else?) the red service stripes are replaced with gold ones.

In my personnel record there are numerous letters of commendation, achievement and appreciation. Also in this file are my semiannual performance ratings. They are excellent. Of course, I wrote my own evaluations for six years. My record also contained six job specialty codes and 35 correspondence courses I had completed.

I loved crisis, and there was a lot of it in military medicine. My 20 years as a hospital corpsman was a rush! I worked in emergency rooms, drove ambulances and flew helicopters doing search and rescue work — this in addition to managing clinics and supervising others. My approach to management was to give 150 percent and "I'll do it so the job is done *right.*" I was rewarded for my workaholism by being assigned more tasks.

Other ACoAs I knew behaved in much the same manner as I. There was a pilot who flew three combat sorties per day when he could have flown two, the acceptable standard. There were many who survived on three hours of sleep or less for days on end in order to meet the *can do* edict of the command.

In my drinking years I looked for a boss who had a drinking problem or another ACoA. I was enabled for years by both. There were many chances to confront me — yet what problem drinker or ACoA would or could violate the *no talk* rule?

During my last year in the service I experienced abandonment. I was transferred from the Navy to the Marines. I had spent 19 years being a good sailor and I felt devastated by this turn of events.

It was also at this time that I first discovered an article concerning Adult Children of Alcoholics. It talked about issues that I had been living with but had not recognized. Once I began to understand them, I could deal with all the other issues in my life. This made my transition from the military to civilian life much easier since I could understand the feelings I was encountering.

4
Boundaries

One of the legacies of growing up in a family affected by alcohol is that there is a blurring of boundaries. This leads to confusion in virtually all areas of adult life. In the workplace it affects relationships with supervisors and peers.

The interaction with parents will transfer to the interaction with supervisors. If you grew up with alcoholism, it was hard to tell who was the parent and who was the child. The child not only had to self-parent but also, in many cases, to parent the parents in order to keep the peace so that things would not get out of control and someone get hurt.

As a result, the ACoA's feelings toward authority are ambivalent at best. Anger and fear, the need to protect the self and to anticipate trouble — these feelings arise regardless of the personality of the supervisor. ACoAs will interpret behaviors of supervisors in this framework with evidence that may or may not be related.

I got a call from my friend Bob, a vice-president of our local bank. "You may like working with these ACoAs," he said, "but, frankly, I don't know if it's worth all the energy. I just had a meeting with my branch manager and I'm still spinning. John came into my office and, out of the blue, announced that he was upset with me. He said, 'You know how strongly I felt about the schedule changes and you don't care about my feelings!'

"I said, 'Wait a minute! That simply isn't true. I supported the schedule changes you wanted *because* I care about your feelings. I don't happen to agree with you but I can understand your point of view and I'm willing to go along.'

"I was completely thrown by what he said. For me, it was a business decision. I was not emotionally invested in it. I can respect points of view other than my own even if I disagree. For me, it was uncomplicated and frankly unimportant in terms of other things that I'm dealing with right now.

"Obviously, it was a big deal for him. He wanted not only my support of his idea but for me to agree that his was the only way to go."

The problem relates to lack of boundaries. The boundaries between him and his idea no longer existed. If Bob didn't agree with John's idea, he didn't care about John.

Bob had also become the parent whose approval he always sought and never got. He was playing out his childhood tape of *Do whatever you want — just leave me alone.*

Even if the employer is aware of all this, it is not his role to *fix it.* If he does that, then he plays into the boundary confusion. His role is to be clear, supportive and consistent. As it happened, Bob got angry because he would not allow himself to be abused and pushing down his feelings would be destructive to him.

Since John sees Bob as a parent, Bob's anger has meaning beyond the interaction. Was he now going to be fired? Did he have to keep a low profile so things wouldn't get worse? Did he have to confront him now about it?

Since the boundaries are so confused, no attention is paid to Bob's position, feelings or reactions and what they mean. The person with boundary confusion gets so caught up in his own feelings and reactions that it is a real struggle to get past them and be aware of what is going on with someone else.

If he can get outside of himself, the branch manager needs to let go of it at this point, because a minor situation is starting to get out of hand. He needs to look at the stuff of the conflict — a change in scheduling design. He wanted the change. The VP was satisfied with the way things were and saw no need for change but would go along with the changes.

The way it progressed was that the situation was not allowed to die. The branch manager wrote Bob a letter about how he reacted to his anger. The VP chose to ignore the letter but couldn't help questioning his judgment as to whether this person's value to the organization was as great as he had believed originally. Managers are supposed to put out fires, not start them.

In families affected by alcohol, sibling relationships get distorted as well. Siblings tend to live side by side and although older kids may take care of younger ones, feelings are not shared and meaningful interaction does not take place. There is not a sense of closeness. They live alone together.

Similarly, the peer relationship in the workplace tends to get confused. The desire to get close along with the fear of discovery results in ambivalence. The role playing (because of the risk of being rejected if you show yourself as you really are — whatever that is) leads to distancing. The question of what is safe to talk about and what is not safe to talk about creates confusion. Too much or too little ends up being said. Wanting to be liked will make the ACoA overly sensitive to disagreeable co-workers or sexual innuendos. The ACoA will also be prone to covering up for slackers and does not know how much to help a fellow worker who is behind.

Julia was upset and confused. Her office mate, Sandy, was always late coming back from lunch and coffee breaks. "I'm furious! I end up answering her phone and taking her messages. It's like I'm *her* lousy secretary. I haven't said anything to her yet because I'm afraid I'll lose control or cry. It's like my family. I'm the only one who ever does anything."

The overwhelming nature of the problem exists because of Julia's lack of understanding of boundaries. Her statement about being *the only one who ever does anything* is the clue. Once again, she is taking over as she did as a child. It's the role she knows. If she had a better understanding of boundaries, she wouldn't have a problem. She simply would not answer the other phone. It is not her problem unless she takes it on as her problem. If the phone goes unanswered, it is Sandy's problem. Sandy then has to deal with the consequences, not Julia.

The reality is that her lack of understanding of boundaries is what makes it a big issue for her and probably what allows Sandy to take advantage: No problem — Julia will cover, she's a dear.

Sexuality In The Workplace

Many ACoAs have been sexually abused as children. This is true for both men and women although women are generally more aware of the experience. As a result, any hint of sexual harassment in the workplace causes a very powerful response. Any inappropriate gesture or remark will provoke either a panic or a battle response.

Although sexual gamesmanship is generally considered undesirable, the ACoA will go after the "perpetrator" with a cannon when a peashooter might have the desired effect. The other extreme of quitting or asking for a transfer may also be an overkill response from childhood.

Needless to say, the promise of promotion for sexual favors is, in and of itself, horrendous enough to warrant whatever power can be harnessed against it. Such "advances" confuse ACoAs, who always wonder if they are over-reacting or minimizing when they are told, "Everybody does it! It's not such a big deal." The discussion here is about the obnoxious office Romeo who propositions everyone rather than someone who pays a simple compliment — "How nice you look today."

Not only is there the early childhood trauma that surfaces in these instances but also a lack of skill in knowing what to say or how to say it in order to get a point across without creating lifelong ill will.

Many EAP counselors who work with ACoAs report that they will tend to have high risk affairs in the workplace. These involve, for example, the married boss. This kind of living on the edge is symptomatic of the ACoA's attraction to excitement, stress and chaos. It also plays into the attraction to someone who is unavailable, so that no real intimacy has to be established. What is established is the fantasy of "He will love me so much that he will leave his wife and we will ride off into the sunset and live happily ever after." Not to worry, though; he won't.

The problem that occurs here is that inevitably the boss gets bored and ends the affair; or belief in the fantasy puts pressure on the relationship and it ends; or the ACoA matures and becomes involved with someone available. And as a result the work environment goes sour.

This is the point at which help may be sought in the form of a complaint at being passed over or a request for transfer. Or the ACoA may be referred to the Employee Assistance Program or fired because of poor job performance.

Once again, the ACoA doesn't know what hit her but is certain the problem exists either wholly outside or wholly inside of herself.

Consideration must also be given to the ACoA who is gay or lesbian. The fear of being found out, the sense of being different, the sense of making yourself up because you don't know who you are — these are symptomatic of being ACoA and are also characteristic of being gay and closeted. These fears are, therefore, doubly powerful.

One of the significant distinctions that compounds the issue is that much of the fear that the ACoA experiences exists only in the emotional world and not in the real world. These fears may lead to certain self-defeating behaviors that create their own consequences but are, for the most part, ACoA-initiated.

For the gay person, the fear of being found out, the sense of being different, the need to manufacture a person because the real you would not be acceptable, exist in the real world. Corporate homophobia is a fact of life and is played out in a variety of subtle and not-so-subtle ways; the person who is gay and also an ACoA ends up extremely confused. Which is my ACoA stuff? Which is my gay stuff? And who the hell am I?

These distinctions need to be addressed by a counselor sensitive to both gay and ACoA issues because eventually the lie becomes confused with the truth and the result is disaster.

5
ACoAs And Workaholism

Workaholism is a condition in which the workplace permeates the consciousness to such an extent that it is difficult to concentrate or think about anything other than work. It is different from enjoying your work in that it has more of the characteristics of an addiction. Work becomes a high, and withdrawal from it can cause nervousness, anxiety and depression. Family and friends are neglected and although at first they encourage you and adjust, eventually they exclude you from their lives.

Working hard by active conscious choice is different from what is being discussed here. The concern here is for those who find themselves in a compulsive pattern that is not satisfying to them, who don't know how they got there or how to break out of the pattern.

Here is one ACoA's description of the workaholic situation:

When I wonder about how I became a workaholic, it is pretty clear that it was all part of a process. I didn't set out to be over involved; it just happened. At work I feel loved, accepted, respected and trusted. These are all strong needs of mine. As these feelings grabbed me, I became more secure and developed a deep sense of loyalty. My trust in these feelings developed slowly over the past four years and nine months.

If I label my role here, I see myself as a *family hero*. There are several *heroes* here, and in some ways we work well together. We're committed to keeping everything running smoothly. We try to anticipate all possible calamities and we fix the screw-ups. We do have problems working together, problems of control. I supervise someone who is also a strong family hero and she is the most difficult person of all to supervise.

Not all the feelings are good ones. I also feel frustration over poor communication, lack of planning, lack of direction and lack of clear expectations. I feel disappointed that others seem willing to be so passive. I feel angry at myself when I react to their passivity by becoming more active and intense.

I know intellectually that if I were not here, it would all go on, that I don't make the difference, but I don't know how not to react. Because of the love and acceptance I feel, I am very committed to what goes on here. As long as I am here, I have to give it my absolute best.

The problem in all of this is the amount of energy it takes. When I am feeling frustrated or angry, I use up so much energy. I also do a number on myself — "You shouldn't feel this way; you should be grateful" — and that moves me nicely into guilt, which depletes me even more.

In the last four years, I've clearly become addicted to this job. I put the bulk of my time, energy, thoughts and emotions into this place. I tell the people I supervise that they and their families come first and then the job but I don't practice this myself. I've let a lot go in these four years. I don't keep up friendships. I want to go out less and less. I've become more introverted and there's not much I talk about that isn't work-related. I'm boring to me. I've been a supervisor now for one year and as a result, I feel more alone because my peer group is now much smaller. I'm less confident and less sure of myself. I've received positive feedback but I don't really accept or believe it.

I feel panicky at times that I've made the wrong decision by becoming a supervisor. I've felt despair because I don't see a good future here and I'm scared because I don't know what else to do. I feel trapped. Like the alcoholic, I feel that everything is slipping away except my addiction to my job. My circle is getting smaller and tighter.

I reached a point where I saw only two alternatives. The first would be to quit; the other was to kill myself. That terrifies me because I don't know what else to do. Fortunately, I don't have such narrow vision that I don't know there are other alternatives — I just need to identify them.

One thing I really don't understand is how after four years of doing well in my job, being promoted and getting good feedback, I still feel so unsure of my future and so lacking in confidence.

I realize the members of the *family* I work with are in various stages of their own recovery, but I feel I'm slipping backward. I don't know how any of this is coming across. I feel confused but I am determined to get more comfortable. I do realize that *only I can change how I feel.* My first goal is to build up my confidence. I want to look at other alternatives and either find a way to become more comfortable here or make whatever change I need to make.

6

ACoAs And Burnout

orkaholism is the first step toward burnout and the ACoA is a natural candidate for burnout. Not knowing what is normal leads to overdoing and overproving. Not knowing limitations leads to *not* saying no. Burnout is a condition that results when an individual gives more than he has to give. A person suffering from burnout feels there is nothing left.

Burnout is characterized by depression and inability to get out of bed in the morning; in loss of or extreme increase of appetite; agoraphobia; a variety of physical symptoms; and substance abuse. You can begin to address the issue of burnout by taking a good hard look at the following questions:

- How much have I taken on?
- How much of it is necessary?
- How much of it is unnecessary?
- What steps can I take to relieve myself of unnecessary responsibility?
- What steps can I take to relieve myself of responsibility which may not be necessary in the real world but only in the emotional world?
- How do I establish priorities?

- How do I balance a day?
- How do I prevent relapse?

Most of us burn out once. But for ACoAs, without intervention, the burnout pattern is to get sick, regroup and then head toward the next burnout.

This happens because it's the only way ACoAs know how to behave. With no understanding of or appreciation for moderation, they think that getting sick is the only way *not* to be in charge. The pattern is predictable.

ACoAs also suffer burnout because of deeper reasons. Part of the survival struggle that the ACoA carries into adulthood propels him toward burnout. It is hard for ACoAs to believe that they have succeeded at anything, that they have made it and so they continue to play out historical issues.

A high-achieving ACoA shares the following feelings in a supervisory group. She has been hanging onto her anger at her parents even though they are no longer living. She has no idea at first that she is about to zero in on why she burns out when she "knows better" — *What's in it for you to stay angry? What is your gain?*

Her answer, profound and painful, makes it clear.

If I hang onto my anger at my parents, I don't have to risk death. If I'm angry, I don't have to risk being close. I don't have to risk growing up. If I grow up and become responsible for myself, I have to give up my search for nurture. I have to take care of myself. Taking care of myself means I will be all alone and if I am all alone, I will die.

So I avoid that by holding onto my anger at my parents as the only route to freedom from them, but I end up locked inside myself. Owning up to the fact that I don't know how to take care of myself is very hard because I know so well how to take care of others.

I *do* and *don't* want to be responsible *to* and *for* myself. I want my independence but I yearn for the nurturing. This is very painful to deal with so I try to reduce the risk of sharing this side of myself.

One of the ways in which I reduce the risk of being responsible is to take on many responsibilities. If I do that, then I don't have to face myself and no one will know because I am super-responsible that that is the way I cover my fear. Being super-responsible to and for others will effectively hide the fact that I'm ignoring my obligation to myself.

This statement of the problem clearly demonstrates why asking the usual questions is not sufficient. In addition to the tools described earlier, it is imperative that you learn how to . . .

- recognize positive feedback
- acknowledge it
- let it in.

Being offered greater responsibility is positive feedback. It may not be in your best interest to take on more but that does not diminish or dismiss it as a "stroke." Sort things out. Be flattered (do it consciously, even if you can't feel it) that you are seen as being capable. Then make a decision based on what *you want* to do. The compliment of being offered a promotion does not mean you have to accept it.

At the first sign of stress, *slow down.* Learn to recognize your earliest stress symptoms. *Prevention* magazine published the following list. Some items may be new to you; you may have others to add.

At the first sign of stress, *SLOW DOWN.* Yes — easy for me to say; almost as easy as *I told you so.*

Minor Symptoms That May Signal Stress

☐ Rashes
☐ More colds than normal
☐ Hives
☐ Memory slips
☐ Concentration slides
☐ Foot or finger tapping
☐ Teeth gnashing, grinding
☐ Awaking at 3 A.M. and being unable to fall back asleep
☐ Appetite disorders (eat too much or lose appetite)
☐ Diarrhea
☐ Heart palpitations
☐ Eyelid twitching
☐ Difficulty falling or staying asleep
☐ Minor back pain
☐ Sudden bursts of energy
☐ Increased sweating
☐ More minor accidents than normal
☐ Flatulence
☐ Frowning/wrinkled forehead
☐ Feelings of suspiciousness, worthlessness, inadequacy or rejection
☐ Anticipating the worst
☐ Nervousness before anything happens
☐ Not recognizing a personality shift and refusing to believe it when pointed out

☐ Cold hands or feet
☐ Halitosis
☐ Rapid heartbeat
☐ Racing thoughts
☐ Feeling trapped
☐ Anger, irritation
☐ Feeling that things are getting out of control
☐ Muscle aches
☐ Allergies
☐ Jaw pain
☐ Minor stomach discomfort
☐ Bloated, full feeling
☐ Constipation
☐ Facial tics, twitches
☐ Slight stutter
☐ Dry mouth
☐ Difficulty swallowing
☐ Nausea, vomiting
☐ Chronic fatigue
☐ Lack of interest in sex
☐ Gain/lose weight
☐ Menstrual distress
☐ Cold, clammy hands
☐ Frequent bouts with flu
☐ Arthritic joint pain
☐ Indecisiveness
☐ Frustration
☐ Anxiety, panic

7
ACoAs As Employees

uch of the inner struggle that ACoAs face in the workplace results from childhood myths. The myths had an effect on how they behaved and felt in the classroom during childhood and in adult life, the myths play themselves out in the work environment.

Myths are a part of a belief system. They substantiate our sense of who we are. The beliefs are internalized and are held onto both consciously and unconsciously. They are the result of childhood messages and unless challenged, they are believed well into adult life. Once these myths are challenged, there is a sense of disbelief for ACoAs, followed by relief that the baggage no longer has to be carried around but giving them up is not automatic. It requires hard work. Some popularly held myths include:

If I Don't Get Along With My Boss, It Is My Fault

There is something wrong with me if I cannot make this relationship go right. There is something wrong with me if my boss doesn't treat me the way I ought to be treated. There is something wrong with me if I cannot relate to my boss.

Then again, maybe it doesn't mean there is something wrong with you. Maybe there is simply something wrong, or maybe there is something wrong with your boss.

The important question is, why, if you cannot relate to your boss and you have tried every way you know how, do you stay? What keeps you stuck? Why not consider working someplace else? The decision to leave a bad situation does not automatically mean you have failed. Recognizing the breakdown of your working relationship may mean that you are beginning to take better care of yourself.

There are many reasons why work situations might be undesirable. You may not get along with your boss and it may not have anything to do with a deficiency in either of you; it may come from philosophic differences that you both are unwilling to compromise. Seeking out organizations that are more in line with your thoughts may make for a healthier work environment for you.

It may also be that your supervisor reminds you too closely of that alcoholic parent whose approval you sought and could never achieve. You judge yourself because you think you should be able to handle it better now that you are in recovery. But why should you have to handle it? Why should you use all that energy to remain stable when you could be using it in ways that will enhance your growth? Leaving a work situation that is unhealthy for you is *not* the same as the *geographic cure* taken by alcoholics.

If I Am Not Productive, I Am Worthless

The worth of a person has nothing to do with productivity. You are worthy simply because you are. This is contrary to your early conditioning, so trying to prove your worth is automatic to you. As a result of therapy, a man I know divested himself of one aspect of his professional responsibilities. It took three people to replace him. He told me that as a child he learned that he simply could not trust his parents to be there for him. He had to take care of himself and they still put him down. They told him that he was no good, he was worthless, he was stupid, he was incompetent. He believed them but he couldn't trust them to help him find ways out of his struggle. So he relied on himself because he couldn't rely on anybody else. Although he couldn't believe in them, he believed their message. As a result, he didn't feel good about himself but continued to have to prove to himself that he was OK because he couldn't trust anybody else to do it.

If I'm Not Suited For The Job I'm Supposed To Be Suited For, There Is Something Wrong With Me

Other people have said you'd be an ideal teacher, or you really should be an administrator, or you really should take this promotion. But something in you says that's not where you want to be, that it doesn't feel right to you. Still, you believe the only reason it doesn't feel right is because there's something wrong with you. You've known for so long that other people know what's best for you, that what's going to feel good exists outside of you, that even if something inside tells you different, you discount it.

Sally was offered the job of head nurse. Everyone said she was ideal for the job, but when she thought about taking it she got sick to her stomach. She said to me, "I want to want the job I'm supposed to want. I just *don't* want it. But I should still go after it because I can't trust my own feelings."

You need to be able to allow yourself to trust your own judgment. Trust and go with it.

You can also make a mistake. Sometimes you are not sure that your fearful reaction is as much to be trusted as other people's opinions of what is best for you. It is hard to sort that out. One of the ways to sort it out is to take a chance. Either it will work out or it won't. There is nothing wrong with you if you decide that the change or promotion does not enhance you. You just need to decide in advance that you will not be stuck. Put the job on probation just as you are put on probation in it. It is hard for anyone to know in advance how a new job will work out. Why should you be any different? You can exhaust yourself trying to make the perfect decision before the fact and that simply isn't possible.

I personally prefer to make a decision, be it right or wrong, and learn from it rather than be indecisive and let life happen to me.

I'm Afraid They Will Find Out That I Am Not Capable Of Doing The Job

It really doesn't matter what your skill level is or what you're doing. If you don't continue to prove yourself, they will find out what you knew all along — that you fooled them, that you really don't know what you're doing.

This is apparent at the college level. The ACoA believes that acceptance to college was through a computer error; the As on your report card only put off the day of discovery. After all, you really don't know what you're doing, you really don't know what you're talking about. This helps propel you toward workaholism because you have to keep the pressure on yourself to keep them from finding you out.

I often wonder how employers in this sophisticated era can be so incompetent as to hire people who are not capable of doing the job for which they are hired — and how they make that error most often with you. Interesting paradox — your manipulative skills are so well developed that they hide your lack of skill on the job. Either your boss is fooled or he is not fooled. If he is fooled, he is foolish enough to continue to believe you are capable. If he is not fooled, he knew what you could do from the beginning.

It's a hard feeling to shake. Feeling incapable and being incapable are very different. Work on separating that out. The early tapes — the early messages you received from your family — address the feeling; but job performance addresses the capability more accurately.

I'm Afraid They Will Find Out That
I'm Not Worthy Of Having This Job

The sense of worth, or rather, lack of it, comes from the same thing that many ACoAs feel. They're going to find out what a disgusting person you are because you were responsible for whatever terrible things went on in your family. If you hadn't been born, everything would've been fine. Although other people may make mistakes, you *are* a mistake. You were told it often enough and now you believe it.

How stressful this is, particularly in a work situation where you are treated with respect and are valued. This will cause you to distance yourself from those very people who offer you the validation you crave. It creates an approach-avoidance conflict that is excruciating. The excitement of making a reality out of your childhood fantasy of getting your needs fulfilled is met head-on with terror that it is going to blow up in your face because you're unworthy.

If I Say No, I Will Be Replaced

So you don't say no. You believe that you are the one person they're not going to have any trouble replacing. At the very moment that you say no, someone will move into your job. You also don't say no because of a lack of knowledge of your limits.

I have clients who don't say no to things that are absolutely outrageous. A client of mine went to visit a relative who was 300 miles away and dying. The boss called her and said, "Hey, we have a deadline to meet." She came back because she didn't know she had the right to say no.

The worst possible outcome of saying no — because what you are doing has priority — is that you will lose your job and that may not be the worst possible outcome.

Anything That Goes Wrong Is My Fault.
Anything That Goes Right, Of Course,
Is The Result Of Fate, Luck Or Chance

Anyone who is unhappy is unhappy with me. This is an emotional response to something that happens in the real world. You know, for example, that the incorrect information in the report was not in your section. You know you were not responsible for it and yet you feel as if you were. You tell yourself that it is crazy for you to feel this way but you can't stop it. The question to ask yourself at this point is: When I was a child, did I get blamed for things that were not my fault? Did I get into trouble when I was nowhere near where the trouble happened? If your answer is yes then you know why emotionally you respond automatically as if you have to defend yourself.

A friend of mine called. "You won't believe this," she said.

"Try me," I replied.

"I just called my mother and she yelled at me for being over an hour late for lunch. I know I had no plans to meet her for lunch but — and here's the kicker — I felt guilty anyway. Does it ever stop?"

Hard to say — certainly being able to laugh about it helps.

Dismissing those things that go right as, "It was easy," or "Anyone could have done it," or "It goes with the territory," or "I just happened to be there" means that you maintain a low self-image. You feel bad about what goes badly regardless of your input and you ignore what goes well, still regardless of your input. Sounds like a pretty stuck place to be.

I Should Be Able To Do Whatever Is Asked Of Me

"Why would my employer ask me to do something unreasonable? Since I don't know what *reasonable* is, I get confused."

Maybe you shouldn't be able to do whatever is asked of you. It is very important for you to learn which requests are reasonable and which are not. The question is not whether or not you are able to fulfill the request but whether it is an appropriate request. One main concern of most of my clients is how they can do less. How can I take on less? How can I make my life less stressful? In my supervisory group, a man under 30 years old had a heart attack that was stress-related. There is no reason for that if you can learn how to put things into perspective. Putting things into perspective can be taught — and can be learned.

Ability is not the key to whether or not you should do something. Nor is "If I don't do it, no one else will." That's one of the traps of your childhood. Is the request consistent with your job description and is it reasonable? That is all that needs to be considered. If you consider that and comply with the request anyway, then it is your conscious choice, which is different from a *should.*

I Shouldn't Have To Ask My Boss For What I Need

That sounds as though bosses should be clairvoyant simply to reduce your risk of not getting your needs met and having to deal with that. The rationale is "I would be invading my boss's space if I asked for what I need." So of course you don't ask. You take care of it yourself, whether it's little or big, whether it's within your domain or not.

One woman shared this observation, "When I ask my boss for what I need, I feel shame . . .

"When I asked my mother for what I needed, she would fall apart and I would feel terrible and end up not only not getting my need met but feeling ashamed. I had inflicted an additional burden on her. As a result, I would end up taking care of her, as well as having to meet my own needs."

Asking for help then becomes a very painful experience. Aside from the predictable difficulty of feeling unworthy of someone else's effort and the sense that I should be able to handle by myself whatever I think I need help with, the fact that my asking will do harm to someone else is what really scares me.

I Should Be Able To Fix It

"I should be able to fix anything and everything that goes wrong." After all, that was your history. You took care of everybody. It is what you know how to do best. "Don't worry I'll . . ." And what happens is that others will let you do it, will often take the credit for what you do, will take you for granted. Unless you get angry enough, you will continue to seek approval in this way. "No sweat, . . . I'll get

the . . . on the way to . . . I'll lay out the money . . . I was staying
late anyway . . . Yours doesn't work; take mine."

The Underachiever

Not all ACoAs are super-responsible, super-achievers who have
been discredited. Many do not begin to approach their potential.
They are held back not by choice but as a response to their
childhood tapes. Many of the tapes are the same as for the super-
achievers but responded to differently.

Sarah, although very capable, goes from one entry-level job to
another. She is never satisfied but that does not change the pattern.

"My mother is a workaholic. All my life people have told me I'm
just like my mother and I hate that. I'm sure that's why I don't try
to achieve. I'm terrified that if I did I would fulfill the prophecy and
end up just like her."

Tom says, "All I ever heard was, 'You're a failure like your father.
You'll never amount to anything.' I guess I believed it. Since it is
inevitable that I will fail, why should I bother? After all, if I don't
try, I can't fail."

That is only part of the risk of succeeding. For Tom the greater
risk is that he will become an orphan, adrift and alone, cut off from
his family. If Tom succeeds, it means violating his life script. It
means his family were liars and that his life has been a lie.

If you are like Tom, you know that in order to continue to be a
member of your family you have to play by their rules. That means
you must fail. If you don't fail, you do not belong. Your bonding
need is so great that the thought of going it alone and giving up that
fantasy of getting your needs met is overwhelming.

Then you further judge yourself because you continue in
patterns that are self-destructive, even though you know better. But
the problem has nothing to do with knowing better. It has to do
with a fear of abandonment.

In the workplace, some of that fear may come from wanting to be
liked and accepted by peers. It is similar to the school-age child
who, even though he knows the answers, doesn't raise his hand so
the others won't think he is a nerd.

There are many who limit their achievement because they will
not give their parents the satisfaction.

"They don't care about me. They only care about what I do. And
that is only so they can brag to others about me. They never tell me."
This self-defeating behavior comes out of anger at your parents.

"I go fast and then I stop dead in my tracks. I don't take the next step because I feel I will die if I do — or I'm taking the next step and I'm doing well and then I do something to sabotage myself."

This is a very powerful response to the childhood message, "You will never amount to anything."

The child within you believes that in going against this message, you are rejecting your parents. Rejecting them means you are all alone. The child in you is afraid that you cannot survive on your own, so it feels as though you are risking death if you continue to grow.

Another variation on this theme is, "All they ever do is nag me about how unsuccessful I am and how well everyone else is doing. I think I don't aspire more just to get back at them."

The reality goes deeper. There is a fear that if they didn't have this to complain about, there would be nothing for them to talk to you about. In fact, the parents do not want the child to succeed for their own unhealthy reasons, and he plays right into their script. It is better to be a loser than to be cut off from the family.

Trying harder, taking aptitude tests, faking it until they make it — these do not work in the long run for the people described here. Support groups and therapy are necessary, first to build a new self-concept and then to learn to behave in accordance with it. Those old messages need to be changed and new ones put in their place. That occurs gradually over time with lots of reinforcement and not without pain. The pain that is experienced happens at the point where the old tape of worthlessness is at odds with the new tape of worthiness. This may be exhausting and depressing.

Recognize ahead of time that this may happen and resolve to overcome it. You cannot allow the disease to win.

ACoAs As Supervisors

The issues for the supervisor who is an ACoA are very similar to, if not the same, as for the employee. They just play out somewhat differently. The way they play out also affects the ACoA's subordinates greatly.

These insecurities lead to management styles that may perpetuate the alcoholic family system. The behavior becomes alcoholic even if drugs are not present. The subordinates become co-dependent. You can create co-dependent responses in subordinates who come from functional families but they will not be as profound as for those who come from dysfunctional families. ACoA supervisors will:

1. Demand Compliance

This is a boundary issue. They become ego involved with their subordinates so they consider any poor performance a reflection on them.

2. Make Changes Overnight

Even though they are replacing someone who hasn't done anything for two years, and even though they probably have a grace period of three to six months before they are expected to make changes, they will push themselves to redesign an entire program within two weeks. Their need is to prove that their appointment was not a mistake so they put undue pressure on both themselves and their subordinates.

3. Want To Be Liked By Everyone

As a result, they will become overinvolved with their subordinates. They will encourage inappropriate self-disclosure and then find themselves in a terrible position when it comes time to rate job performance. The fear of rejection causes them to put off the appropriate confrontation or to handle it poorly. Things either wait until they get out of hand or little things get blown out of proportion. The need to reprimand causes great anxiety.

4. Give Away Their Ego To The Organization

This is another example of a boundary issue.

Jean is a middle-level manager with a small manufacturing company. She has been home with heart palpitations for the last two weeks, and her doctor recommends bed rest for two more. He can find nothing wrong with her heart. She went for a second opinion and the diagnosis was the same: stress reaction.

During the last quarter of last year, the company was in financial trouble. Cuts needed to be made and budgets adjusted to accommodate the difficulty. Jean, a very loyal employee, took those problems on as her own. The company difficulties became hers and the worry totally engulfed her. The company has passed the crisis but she now pays a personal price. Those who worked to solve the problems but did not become emotionally involved with them are now experiencing relief and personal satisfaction.

5. Keep Their Personal Feelings Under Control

Since ACoAs strongly believe that it is vital to keep their personal feelings under control, they keep a lid on them. This is a style that companies support. As a result, managers do not develop their own support systems and suppress their feelings; as I like to put it, they stuff their reactions. It is not unusual for physical symptoms to emerge, such as flushing, heart palpitations, tightness in the jaws and throat, ulcers and colitis.

6. Have A Need For Perfection

This need causes ACoAs to consider performance lacks, such as lateness, on the part of employees as a reflection on them. So they over-react. The subordinate needs to be held accountable for his behavior. Very often he is treated as if the behavior does not exist because the supervisor, internalizing the problem, believes that because he didn't come up with the right formula to fix it, the behavior is his fault.

Although they delegate responsibility, ACoA supervisors tend to be unable to let go and they over-(micro)manage. They do not trust that others will do what they agreed to or will not do it well enough or they back off completely as an overcompensation for their fear.

7. Become Enablers

They often feel responsible for the well-being and survival of their subordinates. As a result, they accommodate and cover up for poor performance. This sets their subordinates up to have unrealistic expectations, be manipulative, and lower their job performance. It places an added burden on the rest of the work group.

The self-feelings of the worker and the self-feeling of the supervisor lead to certain management styles. These behaviors on the part of the supervisor and the reaction on the part of the worker are apt to reproduce the alcoholic family system.

Management Style	Co-dependent Response
Overcritical. Nothing is good enough. A flaw will always be found. Praise is withheld.	"I want him/her to like me. Next time, I'll be good enough."
Overdemanding. Swamps self with work. Swamps employees with work. Expects it done in unrealistic time.	"He wouldn't ask me to do it if he didn't think I could do it. I'll prove I'm worthy."
The promiser.	"This time he means it."
Workaholic or incompetent.	"I need to take care of him/her."
Demeaning. "You're paranoid. You're making a big deal out of nothing. How can you be so stupid?"	"If I had his/her pressures I'd probably react the same way. He wouldn't say it if there wasn't at least a grain of truth in it."
Laissez-faire.	"If I was important enough, he'd pay more attention to me. If I don't have full and complete instructions, I'll screw up."
Rescuing.	"He will understand my pressures and problems, and I don't have to worry if I let certain things go."

⑨
How The
Work Crisis Arises

J n today's work environment change is the norm rather than the exception. Many who have adapted successfully to a work situation that has had some stability and predictability — either chaotic or peaceful — find themselves confronted with changes they did not anticipate or prepare for. When this occurs, many people who have functioned effectively and felt effective find themselves incapable of adapting to the change. They become anxious and respond in ways that are not in their self-interest. As a result they find themselves in emotional and/or job jeopardy. They are not aware of anything they can do to adapt effectively. They do not have the skills necessary to deal with what is happening. People in this position, if they are forced to implement change, will be in crisis.

Some people who have been effective in the work environment may suddenly find that, for no logical reason, they are no longer effective. No matter how hard they try, they are unable to understand why this is happening.

Some of the explanations that follow may help you to get a handle on the cause of the problem and help you find a way to deal with it.

Since the work life is critical to one's well-being and since the workplace for many is a home away from home, it is important to understand the emotional significance of the workplace in order to understand the significance of a crisis in the workplace.

The way you perceive the workplace is directly connected to your self-perception. If the feedback you are given in the workplace is that you belong, have value, and are important, you internalize the message *not* that your career is going well but that you are safe in life. When change occurs in the workplace, you do not experience it as "the job has changed" or "the career has to be reevaluated" but that you are unsafe and at risk in life. This dynamic is the direct result of your history. It will have occurred in similar circumstance in the past where there were peers and authority figures and a sense of needing to be dependent in order to belong. This would have been the dynamic in your family of origin or in your foster care family.

People spend a lot of energy trying either to duplicate early life experience or to ward it off. As a result many find they seek out crisis-laden situations while others seek out situations where they feel very safe. The first person would be in personal crisis if he found himself in a super-safe environment and the second would not be able to handle a chaotic environment. The switch for either would be profoundly painful.

The circumstances that follow are changes that, for many, precipitate a crisis in the workplace.

Promotion

One of the reasons why people are promoted is that they have the ability to interact with their fellow workers in a way that creates a minimum amount of conflict and to read and respond to their fellow workers' needs. People will be rewarded for this ability because management believes that they can take on more responsibility. For some, those abilities are the result of career choice. For others, those behaviors come from a need to minimize conflict and always to be on top of things in order not to experience the painful dissonance of their childhood.

If you are made a supervisor and part of the criteria for advancement is based on those dynamics, you are put into conflict. The role of the supervisor is one that carries with it built-in dissonance with one's subordinates. People who are anxious about relating in this dissonant way will be thrown off balance. Pleasing your boss will now mean stressful relationships with your subordinates because the relationship has a built-in adversarial component.

For some, this level of responsibility is unmanageable. The playing out of history and the resulting disequilibrium cause the crisis. Upper management is now left with the question, "John Jones seemed so good — why didn't it work out when we promoted him?"

Many large companies offer educational experiences to deal with the transition from line-level worker to supervisory level, or supervisory level to upper management, but they do not address these dynamics. The focus in these programs is on helping the new supervisor to develop skills involved in motivating and evaluating employees and on disciplinary techniques, but most programs do not address the new supervisor's need for remedial help in managing the internal dissonance.

When you are promoted and now direct a team, you are in a parent position relative to your former co-workers. When others are now looking to you for evaluation, direction, approval or as a place to act out anger — and your need is to avoid conflict — several things may happen.

If a subordinate is dysfunctional and your family role is to take care, then you feel at risk if that person doesn't make it. If a team reports to you and someone on that team is in a position of not making it, your history will make you feel the need to rescue. The need to rescue will be automatic and will take precedence over how you see yourself vis-a-vis the supervisory role. You will do everything you can in order to allow that employee to continue to survive, which is to say you will enable him, rather than demand that he produce. Because of your own emotional needs, you are unable to allow yourself to find out if your employee, under pressure, can function without your protection.

Supervisory enabling is a common problem on the worksite. Supervisors will take employees who are not capable of doing the job under their wing and because of their own need will (1) rescue them and give them special projects, (2) have others cover for them, and (3) not tell management what is going on. The supervisor will continue in this pattern because of his own need and will be powerless to do otherwise. A supervisor may have a team of ten with four dysfunctional members whom he constantly rescues as a result of his own need.

A supervisor could have had tremendous rage at her own parent and feel that if she does something to her subordinates that might provoke them to anger, they would have the same rage toward her that she has toward her parents. This creates a great deal of anxiety and gives the subordinates a great amount of power. The supervisor will bend over backward not to do anything to cause them anger or disapproval. In a work setting, this dynamic makes it hard to enforce standards.

The typical enabling supervisor will yell and scream a warning, "I will fire you" or "They will dock you," but every time limits are set, the supervisor will back down. In relatively short order, subordinates do not feel any pressure to perform.

Those who do perform become exploited by the workers who are being enabled — for example, having to cover for an active alcoholic — and morale becomes low.

The crisis will surface if, for example, a company is bought out and efficiency experts are sent in and discover that the supervisor's work team is not producing up to standard. The supervisor is suddenly forced to change his style of managing based upon these investigations but is powerless to do so. This happens because it is not a work-related dynamic. He now has to face his rage at those people putting demands on him to "kill off" the people he is responsible for.

As long as production is not a company concern, the practice of enabling can perpetuate itself. When a higher level of management starts looking at how many people are required to do a particular task and then tells the supervisor that he should be running his unit with X number of people when he is running it with $X + Y$, a crisis is precipitated. He will discover that he cannot run it with X number because he "needs" to carry Y number of people. But his need is emotional, not professional, and he does not have to address it until he is challenged. The supervisor cannot produce by using the criteria demanded by the level over him. This will put the supervisor in crisis because he cannot emotionally eliminate his deadwood.

Change In The Job Role

If you have a role in the workplace, you are rewarded for performance related to that role. If that role changes, the criteria for reward change, and the changes cause dissonance.

For many people, a shift in role means a shift in responsibility and new responses to be learned. If your need is to perform perfectly and your need for acceptance is absolute, there will be great anxiety if your ability to be perfect is threatened. If you find a niche where the supervisor is super-supportive, then you don't have to be anxious. You have found a safe place where you are respected.

When the role is changed, the transition puts you at risk because you no longer feel safe. The transitional point is the crisis.

For many people there is also profound loss involved. When you have finally found a place of psychic comfort and learn that that place is going to be disrupted, the reaction goes deeper than that of going from one job to the next. The feeling of loss of the safe family is profound.

Change In The Authority Structure

When people have had a relationship with an authority figure in which they have felt safe, they develop certain fantasies around that relationship. They become somewhat rigid in the response patterns that work and they feel appreciated even if the appreciation is not stated in so many words. When there is a shift in supervisors and the new supervisor is more demanding, there is invariably the complaint, "I'm not appreciated anymore."

Even if the former relationship was silent, there was a sense of being valued. Now when the new supervisor has different criteria for approval or exhibits behaviors reminiscent of dysfunctional parent behaviors, the person is at risk. The person no longer feels safe and is back to the anxiety level he felt in childhood when he was not emotionally safe.

The individual may have become rigid in her behaviors and response pattern in order to ward off the anxiety. If the behaviors are no longer acceptable, it is difficult to give them up and behave in new ways.

If you have a supervisor who makes you feel safe, you will develop a profound loyalty. The loyalty also makes you feel comfortable and nurtured. As a result, you are at extreme risk if the supervisor leaves. You then fantasize that the company is no longer safe. If they got rid of the supervisor, "What is to stop them from getting rid of me next?"

Change In The Organization Itself

Some people enter an organization and stay based on personal dynamics. If you enter an organization that is highly competitive and the criteria to survive is to beat out others and you thrive on that, then change in the organization means that the reason for entering no longer is the same as the reason for staying.

If you learned as a child to survive in this way and it has continued to work for you, you will not be able to utilize feedback around necessary behavior change in the new environment. If you need to be in a competitive, warlike mode to ward off your anxiety about being swallowed up and it is the only way you know how to be separate, you will be fine as long as the environment remains constant.

If the environment changes and there is an attempt toward order and harmonious interchange, you will not fit. It is too painful to be in an environment without contention. You need to fight in order to maintain your uniqueness.

An example of this is the labor organizer who is at the top of his form agitating for change but, when change occurs and he is charged with keeping the hard-fought-for harmony, he will be very unhappy.

The reverse is also true. When you have entered a safe, nurturing, paternalistic environment, a change in the organization in which management becomes more structured or demanding brings up feelings of profound loss. You experience the loss of a safe family and loss of being able to allow the nurture and you feel rejected. If, for example, you're working for an airline and you have to work twice as many flights, or have fewer sick days, you may find that what you have been doing all along is not acceptable. You will then find yourself in crisis. You are back in your nonsupportive family of origin and not in the caring place you allowed yourself to need.

When organizations are fatter, you feel loved and safe; when they trim down and make demands, there is a feeling of vulnerability and fear of being abused. The response is personal and not professional. It is not possible for you to reason that the company's survival necessitates the change. You are only able to tune in to your own loss.

Many organizations, given adverse economic conditions, need to lay off employees. In many instances people who are laid off are closely connected to people still at work. The people who remain are very much aware of the consequences to the people who are laid off, and that awareness directly affects their attitude at work.

Many organizations that have cared for their people attempt to address the issue of layoff. They have out-placement programs and they help people do their resumes. However, some people cannot respond to the organization's effort to offer them practical ways of reintegrating economically.

These people are in crisis because of the loss of the family and early feelings of betrayal are opened up. They have no resources to combat the crisis . . . There is a sense that it is the end of the world and as a result, they become immobilized. Their first successful trust experience may have been at work so they have no prior experience to call upon to help them through the crisis. They will be unable to cope.

The survivors can also become dysfunctional. The workplace feels like a wake. It's the guilt of the survivor. Some survivors become bitter and upset even though they previously felt comfortable and nurtured. At the time they need to make the attitude switch, they are unable to look at the organizational survival needs. They see the organization as a person who threw out their friend. They also fear that they will be next. They can no longer afford to feel safe and nurtured and as a result react in the workplace as they did in their dysfunctional childhood. The organization was "good parent" and is now "bad parent." They know no other way to respond. As a result they become maladaptive.

Sometimes an organization will shift and the shift will not be in the best interest of its workers. If the changes are to build, to sell or if the organization is being milked, some will notice and protect themselves careerwise. Others will notice but, in order to ward off the pain of loss and betrayal, will insist upon missing these cues and continue to be loyal despite the signals that suggest betrayal. They will stick it out to the end.

Change In Personal Life

A change can occur in your personal life that makes you feel unsafe and as a result, you cannot perform effectively at work. People who struggle to have the perfect home life and the perfect work life feel that when something happens in their home life they are at risk in the workplace as well. The inability to be perfect at work causes such anxiety that it puts them in crisis.

Mary's job was to be the liaison between a major company and the public. She did it wonderfully well. As a child her role was to keep peace in the family. Her parents had a troubled marriage, and it was up to her to keep them together. Mary's husband left her without warning. Even though the marriage offered her little, she was devastated. She experienced herself as a failure at keeping things together. This resulted in her feeling like a fraud at work and she became immobilized.

The dynamic occurs when work and home life are similar. If they are different, the job performance may not suffer but there will be a projection onto fellow workers and supervisors of, for example, rejecting behaviors.

John felt marginal as a child — he never felt that he really belonged. He was under fire at work, which brought up the early feelings and as a result, he became aggressive and defensive in the work environment and put himself further at risk.

Frustration Of Career Goals

If you have an inordinate need to be appreciated or acknowledged because you were so unappreciated or were not acknowledged as a child, you will look for ways to gain that appreciation and acknowledgment as an adult. The workplace can be an ideal place for you to meet these needs.

If your supervisor is encouraging and supportive, there is the expectation that the support will translate into support for your advancement as a token of the appreciation. When the fantasy is not realized, then you question the appreciation. Was it fraudulent? He never meant it. She was lying to me.

If the positive things the supervisor says are translated in a way that you think you can trust and then the supervisor does not support an effort toward promotion, your trust is violated and you have a sense of betrayal.

If your family role was to take care of everybody but they were so dysfunctional that you could not do that and you had to make up for them, then you will find in the work environment that you must be perfect to make up for the imperfections of others. When there is an offer of promotion, it causes a crisis because you feel you are abandoning this family of failures. You need to be the savior. As a result it is not unusual to sabotage the promotion. You may screw up tests, not show up for interviews, and the like. Since this is unconscious behavior you will be flabbergasted when the promotion does not come through.

If your career goal is thwarted and career is your only way of feeling potent, if ambition is a reaction to deep feelings of impotence, then a crisis in upward mobility can result in impotence in intimate relations. If this feeling comes from lack of early nurture and you regress, you will not be capable of feeling a bond with your present family. As a result, you cannot use any attempts on the part of the family to offer nurturance. You simply cannot respond. The family will feel rejected at a time when they believe they are most needed. This will also put the family in crisis and compound the dysfunction.

Some who have internalized messages of not being good enough but who still strive to achieve will sabotage success, create crisis where it did not exist before and maintain symbols of not having made it even if they have. An example is a man who develops a good business but contracts with services that don't come through consistently, so he is always in a struggle. It's like living on the edge. It's the only way he can be faithful to his family and to himself.

Difficulty With Peer Relationships

If you have a certain way of belonging with peers and that role shifts, the shift can create a crisis. If you are considered a strong team member and as a result are given more responsibility, you feel at risk if your need is to do well but not stand out. If the additional responsibility causes a shift in your peer relationships and you become more visible, you will then fear disapproval and be anxious because you are not sure how to respond.

If you are an advisor to your peers and a new person who threatens that role comes on the scene, the same anxiety results.

PART TWO

Developing
Healthy Patterns

The problem has been stated. The complexities have been exposed. The next question is "What can be done about it?" Or as the typical ACoA would say, "Is there any hope?"

The answer is simple — yes. There is hope. And yes — there is a great deal that can be done about it.

This section of the book contains the *how to* of unhooking from the past and living in the present, all the while being mindful of the future.

10
Getting Through
The Work Crisis

This section is designed to get you through the crisis so that you will not sabotage yourself when you are going through it. It will help you in three ways:

1. You *won't* have the additional problems you created to deal with, as well as adjusting to the external change.
2. You *will* be able to make rational decisions as to what you want to do in your work life in both the short run and long run.
3. You *will* be able to see that it is a *work* crisis, not something else.

The very first step is to sort out the problem. You need to recognize what the work problem is and what the emotional block is. This is difficult to do because when the crisis happens, it is so all-consuming that there is no energy left to see that you are responding irrationally. Even if you cannot see how irrational you are, you may be able to experience your unmanageability. If you can see your reactions and they are different from your former reactions, you can use that as an indicator of crisis. If you are beginning to act in ways that are alien to a prior successful pattern and if a part of you is fully locked into that way of reacting, that is another indicator. If you experience pain or anxiety or rage or are acting out bitterness or resentment or if you start drinking a lot and that pattern began at the same time that something happened at work, those are also indicators.

At that point, something somewhere has to alert you and say, "Watch out!" — because you no longer have any options that help you protect yourself and act in your *economic* self-interest. Those signals are tough to catch because you're not looking for them. If you don't look in the mirror, you don't know that your nose is red. If there is no part of you that can sort this out and identify this pattern, there is no way to monitor it.

You may be getting external cues that indicate something is wrong. They may come in the form of feedback from other people. If people always said·certain things about you and they continue to give the same message, then nothing has changed. But if people who used to see you one way are giving you feedback indicating a change, that's the time to give some credence to that feedback. It is the time to wonder if you have a handle on your reactions. You then need to begin to think about protecting yourself. Chances are you will not feel motivated to change. You will feel completely and totally justified in your reactions. You will want to fully protect your present style because not to do so would be very painful. You will therefore resist experiencing that level of pain.

All you need do at this point is acknowledge that there *is* a work crisis and that you are resisting recognition of it. Step 1 of the AA program applies here: *I am powerless over my reaction to the work crisis and my life has become unmanageable.*

Allow Another Viewpoint To Exist

Allowing another viewpoint to exist means allowing another perception to have possibilities. This is very difficult to do when you are reacting to deep emotional pain.

You have to know yourself in order to know how to manage this step because different people do it differently. It is a step in which you are very vulnerable and you have to be ready to be good to yourself. You have to expect pain but allow yourself to exist in the current world, separate from your regressed state, which is a powerful reaction to a painful time.

If you don't react well to feedback from other people but are able to manage a more distant feedback, you might attempt a visit to a religious organization or consult with someone who represents a religious persuasion. Allow the input to come from a source that is as consistent in its position as possible.

If you respond well to self-help groups, there are many that you can join in order to begin directing your energies toward looking at another perspective.

You are fragile and you need to receive the input in the way that is most palatable to you. You need the input to be presented in the way that is least emotionally loaded for you. For some people, talking to friends and leaning on people becomes the way. This works for people who are capable of being somewhat dependent. For some people, going to a person who represents a religious organization is more tolerable. It doesn't mean one way is any better than the other. The way you choose is the way that works best for you.

There are people who, faced with a work crisis, will develop a profound connection with a rigid ideology as a way to cope. That is another way to do it. It is a way not to feel the psychic pain and to feel bonded. The bonding with the ideology makes the person feel complete. The result is that you are less fully invested at work. The energy that was previously invested at work is invested in a place that gives nurturance and comfort. Your need to react to the workplace in a better way can be easier because you have a place where you can feel connected.

The point is that when you are faced with a work crisis, it is important for you to acknowledge that you need to distance a little from the situation at work in order to see it for what it really is and you need to find another place to be connected to or another idea to feel connected with.

If your need for meaning was fully satisfied at work, there may be no other place you can see that has any meaning. You may have to test out one of the options offered here as a leap of faith. If something else can become significant, then you can have some free energy to look at work more realistically. There is then movement away from defining yourself as your work. It can mean relating to family or to an association differently. It is similar to the recommendation of 90 meetings in 90 days for the newly sober person so that he can be connected with something other than alcohol. You take the cotton out of your ears and put it in your mouth. Step 2 of the AA program applies here: *[We] came to believe that a Power greater than ourselves could restore us to sanity.*

Change Your Responses At Work

Once you have completed the second step and have developed some meaning in life outside of the work environment, you need to begin to change your behavior in very simple ways. Changing your behavior at work does not mean correcting it. It does not mean changing it radically. It simply means to begin to react more neutrally at work. If you are capable of doing it, it may mean behaving the way you did before you were in crisis. If you were functional beforehand and you can return to that and behave that way, you have accomplished a great deal. If the wound is still pretty deep and, as you begin to look at work, the situation is just beginning to clear up, you may only be able to be neutral. You may have to be able to stay neutral before you can once again live effectively at work. In order to neutralize the situation, you need to look around, get the picture, talk to people outside of work about what you are seeing. You need to connect with people with whom you can talk about what you are seeing, so that you can understand what is going on in work terms instead of emotional terms. You have to be able to take a look at the work environment in a way that has to do with your career and your survival, *not* your feelings. You are, in effect, relearning how to connect with work. You are learning how to do it in a way that has to do with career and money — not with emotional need.

If you are a supervisor who is enraged at upper management and are expressing your anger by telling your subordinates how lousy the company is because you feel pained about needing to shift the rules, you need to stop doing that. You are going to want to just be neutral about things — not to be fully effective but just to be neutral. Stop complaining to upper management and stop demeaning the workplace to subordinates.

Stop doing things to invite a fight. Stop doing things that would suggest personal rage at what has happened. Simply stop that behavior. If you're not handing in your work, to get even — or you're not producing as well, to get even — or you are coming in late, to get even — or you're terribly upset a lot and have a tight pain in your stomach — interrupt that kind of behavior. That behavior does not serve your best career interest. You don't have to feel differently. Just behave differently. Try to keep work at work.

If you are feeling physical symptoms like stomach cramps, headaches or nausea, try to develop strategies to manage these symptoms, for example, relaxation strategies, exercise — things to minimize the new behavior that is related to the work crisis. Recognize that acting out will only sabotage you in the future and make the crisis worse. If you stop complaining, if you stop being hostile, that does not mean you now agree with policy. It just means you are going to act in the way that is in your best interest.

You are intentionally establishing a neutral zone. You are not signing a peace treaty. You create the neutral zone so you won't do something that will cause you to pay dues in the here-and-now and you maintain the zone until you can reframe your understanding of what happened at work.

It might be that as you take a second look at your work situation, you will find new options emerging.

You may decide that this company is not for you. Your best interest may be served in starting to write a new resume. You may consider taking early retirement. If your decision is based on input from other people and on examining what's going on in your career, then just pulling back and making a decision doesn't mean you have to take action. You may decide to hang in and ride out the storm. It simply means you are looking at what makes the most sense in terms of what you need.

Seeing it in these terms is different from the way you saw the workplace in the beginning. In the first place you saw work as your family. If you decide that leaving your family is acting in your best interest, a basic need is violated: to stay connected with your family.

The workplace should not be your home away from home. In some ways you may, as a result of the crisis, be developing a new skill. It may be very painful because you may feel disloyal. You may feel you don't deserve to act in your own interest. Those feelings will come up now. Be ready for them. It may not be possible to take action at a time when you are dealing with such a painful experience. At this point, all you need do is just examine what action would be in your best career interest.

Look at the situation with someone who can help you do it in an objective way. It is too emotionally loaded for you to do it by yourself. If you have friends who are objective, they can be very useful at this time. Do not pick friends who are (1) as angry as you are and will direct you to do something for their rage, or (2) who clearly identify with you because they have a similar history and may guide you to act out their fantasies. These friends may not be able to be objective because they care too much about you and what you're going through to see things clearly.

This is the time to take an objective look and incorporate objective people. If you have people in your life who are objective and whose career perception is clear, they may be able to help. It may be the time to see a professional who can offer an objective point of view. If you choose to go to a professional, be sure the professional you go to is one who will be reality-oriented and will help you work on your current situation. The professional for this time is someone who is going to help see the decisions you need to make around the workplace. He may help you link here-and-now and the there-and-then in order to help you focus on the workplace. His help will not be focused on your history as it relates to the workplace but to your current situation. At another time you may want to focus differently, but for now, in the crisis, this is appropriate focus.

As you look at the workplace more objectively and with the help of someone objective, you can anticipate some pain, some automatic rejection of ideas and some denial. Looking at the situation more objectively brings you another step further away from the emotional need that existed initially. It is important not to judge yourself because it is so hard for you to see the situation objectively. If you could have looked at it objectively from the beginning, you would have. If your early life experience and those emotions had not interfered, you probably would not be in a crisis this severe.

Take your time. If you've been able to maintain a functional mode, you now have time. As a result of this process you can now look at action options. You are now not only looking objectively but a little more deeply. What does this mean for me here? Is this the place where I want to continue to work? Is this the place where I need to be? Looking objectively, what are my goals? Am I better off leaving or am I better off staying? Do I want to maintain the role that I had prior to the crisis? Was that role good for me? Are there ways for me to modify my role? There are many options when the pressure is off.

If you now find it desirable to invest some energy outside the workplace, you may decide to invest less energy at work. You may decide not to quit but to shift your energy a little. Looking at goals gives you a chance to explore the whole picture and lets you see objectively what it was like before. When you were in crisis you were facing the pit that you avoided all your life. Now you're in a position to see what you did in order to adapt.

The crisis does not have to be seen only as an enemy. It can also be seen as an opportunity. You may have been stuck and can now get unstuck.

The initial goals you should identify are short-term goals. But looking at short-term goals can also afford you an opportunity to look at your long-term goals and how the two relate. If you are the adult child of an alcoholic, chances are you have never really looked at long-term goals or known how to develop a long-term plan. So one of your short-term goals might be to learn how to develop long-term goals.

Once you have examined your goals, you won't feel obligated to make a change. As long as you're functional at work, you still have the luxury of maintaining your neutral stance while you explore your options. You may decide to stay put for a year and maintain your *status quo*. You may not want to make a major decision for that period of time. In effect, you have achieved a goal for a year. You can be free to enjoy other things. Along the way you may have many questions but you've done what you need to do for now. You will live crisis-free.

Recognize that living crisis-free may in itself require an adjustment on your part.

If your life is crisis-oriented and that is how you live your life, that is a crisis with a small *c*. If you continue to have crisis as you have known it before, that is a part of who you are. The Crisis — with a big *C* — that we are talking about is a reaction to an event that causes you to behave uncharacteristically and self-destructively. If having a crisis is the norm for you, then *not* having a crisis would be a crisis. If functioning at work is your norm or having a certain role at work is your norm and that gets shifted, then the crisis is related to that. And that's a Crisis with a big *C*.

This distinction is something you may begin to filter out in going through this process. The two kinds of crises may feel somewhat the same inside but in reality they are different. We usually use the term *crisis* to mean being in situations where we feel anxiety or a sense of imminent danger. But in this context, we are talking about something different. The crisis in the workplace results from an event that causes an uncharacteristic set of behaviors or feelings. It is not necessarily a crisis that makes the adrenalin start to flow.

There are a lot of people whose lives are a mess but who do well at work. There are a lot of people who are continually in difficulty at work. They constantly act out at work in ways to ward off early pain. They are always late or in some difficulty with authority figures. For some, these dysfunctional patterns are the norm. If you behave regularly in this way, you will discover that interrupting the pattern has a different flavor. In that event, you might need to look at what in your psychological make-up is causing you to behave this way and emphasize this aspect, rather than the particular work crisis of the moment.

Recognizing Your Work Style

Here is another way of looking at the meaning of crisis in the workplace. You are reading this and maybe wondering, "Where do I fit? I always have crisis at work. Why don't I identify with what is being said?"

It might be that, affected by your childhood, your style or the way you relate to your current work environment makes you crisis-prone and that is your norm. It is important that you understand how this section relates to you as well. You may be constantly in pain about work. You may be always in conflict with your boss. You may keep losing jobs and not understand why. The job loss does not relate to an inability to do the work but to an inability to relate to others. If you can't do the work because of lack of skill, you may be able to learn to do the work by getting training. If you are unable to relate at work but have the skill, then there's something else going on. If these problems are true for you, you may be crisis-prone at work. Your situation is different from that of the person who doesn't usually feel appreciated but finds a way to behave at work that is appreciated. When one is feeling functional at work and then the crisis hits, it is not the same as if you . . .

- constantly feel unappreciated and angry and act out
- constantly feel the boss is out to get you, no matter who the boss is
- constantly walk around with the feeling that if you haven't done everything perfectly, something terrible will happen
- constantly feel at risk
- constantly quit jobs because you feel unsafe.

This situation may not be a work crisis. It may be a personal crisis that plays itself out at work. You have to take a look at the patterns and the way in which you play out your internal problems at work. You may have to think back on each time you insisted that this boss was lousy or that boss was lousy or this organization stinks or that organization stinks. It may make sense for you to sit down and see if there are any patterns to your actions. If there are, ask yourself whether or not something you are doing is the cause.

It may be your attitude or your choice of employment. You don't have to be angry at yourself if you find that to be the case. It means that it may be worth your while to sit down in a safe, quiet place and give it some thought.

The remediation process that has been described here is not necessarily appropriate for you if you fall into this latter category. If you do, you might want to take a look at the myths and other areas discussed in other parts of this book in order to more fully identify what it is that you are playing out at work.

For most of you, both of these aspects will have validity at one time or another.

As long as the workplace has the same stability for you that it has always had, this book may not be useful to you because you have succeeded in warding off the pain from the past and feel safe and functional. The crises we have talked about remedying are those that are caused by circumstances out of your control and those that, because of your history, you lack the tools to respond to appropriately. This section is designed to help you develop those tools.

One caution: Don't rush to act on an idea or make a change you believe is needed unless your job is at imminent risk.

If the need to change is not immediate, chances are that whatever decisions you make should be held up or slowed down for careful planning. It will take a while for everything to quiet down so that you can make a decision you are certain will not backfire. Let the dust settle.

Start to look at new career options in a realistic way. Read about changing jobs. Give yourself time. The crisis in the workplace has all the power of a trauma and you need time to heal from a trauma. Exploring new career options requires different skills and thought patterns, different modes of operation, different affiliations. The skills needed to get through the crisis are not the same as the skills needed to explore new career options. You need time to learn those skills, if the workplace gives you time to plan.

Don't tell anyone at work that you're thinking of leaving. Keep that outside of the work site. The decision to leave does not mean that you have failed where you are. It just means that you may need to make a decision to leave.

You may decide you can advance your career where you are. Give yourself time to be where you are. Then look carefully at what would serve your interest in that direction. You may decide that where you are, now that you are adjusting, is precisely where you want to be.

You may want to look at early retirement. You may want to go back to school. You may want to do something entirely different.

All things are possible when you've passed the crisis. Working it through not only helps you survive in the moment but can ultimately be enriching. As the AA program tells you — one day at a time — one step at a time. It gets better.

11
Changing Jobs

CoAs do not accept change easily. Change, regardless of its nature, involves loss. The sense of self is tentative and for many, the personal identity and the work identity are one and the same, so any change in the workplace is disruptive. It involves the loss of self as it has been understood by the ACoA. Many find themselves in tears when things are going well and devastated when things are going poorly. Identification with occupation is not exclusive to ACoAs but the exaggerated reaction to change is relevant.

Leaving a job is stressful to the ACoA because leaving is a sign of disloyalty, so the ACoA will experience guilt.

ACoAs believe that former colleagues . . .

- will be angry with them
- won't like them anymore
- will punish them

They also believe that the new colleagues . . .

- will reject them, so they will be alone in a hostile environment.

If the ACoA takes care of himself, he believes something terrible will happen to others.

- Those who were under my protection will be thrown to the wolves.

It's called survivor guilt.

For many, the leaving is more difficult than the new start. That is not only because of the struggles involved in leaving but also because focusing on the leaving serves as a smokescreen to avoid the fears involved in the change, including (1) fear of success and (2) fear of failure.

Much has been written about the female fear of success (nice girls don't) and the male fear of failure (if you're a man, you will succeed), and those culturally defined fears exist for the ACoA as well. In and of themselves the messages "You'll never get a man" or "The world will know you're a wimp" can cause you great anxiety.

However, for the ACoA, the underlying message "You're not worthy" and the unconscious belief in that message cause panic when the ACoA attempts change.

The decision to change jobs is excruciating for an ACoA because the ACoA lacks decision-making skills. The ACoA has no frame of reference for making a careful, thought-out decision without help.

It is not unusual for an ACoA to get stuck in trying to make a decision. This comes from forward and backward projection and an inability or lack of understanding of necessary steps in the moment.

Since leaving is so hard, it has to be the perfect job. It has to be the right location, the right title, the right job description, the right salary, the right perks, the right opportunity for advancement, the right assistance — in short, everything. Otherwise, why bother? The agonizing over leaving means that the new job is a life-long commitment. The idea that the company might change, that you might change or that what is ideal for you today may not be ideal tomorrow is too complicated a notion to enter the picture.

Changing jobs involves learning, and learning involves risk. This brings up the childhood fears, "If I take a risk and it's a mistake, my parents will humiliate me, mock me and make fun of me to their friends." The memory of that torture is excruciating.

In general people look for new jobs because they are unsatisfied where they are, a growth opportunity presents itself, it is time to move on for one's own development, or circumstances intervene.

As a result of the ACoA's decision-making problems, his job changes will often happen to him, rather than result from the ACoA making the decision. Whether the decision to change jobs is his own or someone else's idea, the ACoA is prone to make impulsive decisions and live with the results of those impulses.

ACoAs look for a new job when the present situation becomes intolerable. Dissatisfaction is generally rationalized or dismissed or blamed on self. Subsequently, the discomfort builds until the situation is intolerable. Then the ACoA must find another job or he will create additional problems for himself or get fired. The result is that the search is made with great urgency and a new position becomes more the luck of the draw than a carefully selected choice. This rapid choice is a good way for setting up the same situation all over again.

Even though the ACoA complains that she is under-appreciated and under-utilized, she does not meet growth opportunities with enthusiasm and an inner self-validation. The ACoA meets them with fear of discovery on the one hand and, on the other, the suspicion that any growth opportunity is not all that it appears to be. Since most new opportunities are not all they're purported to be, looking at the negative side helps to allay the inadequacy fears. It is a sign of growth for the ACoA to address concerns directly and discuss terms. It is more usual to stuff concerns, put off the decision, panic that someone else will be offered the job and end up accepting the job on the employer's terms. Losing the opportunity as the result of avoidance is an alternate possibility and leads to an initial sense of relief. Then the fantasy of *if only* sets in.

ACoAs rarely move on solely because it is time to go further. This comes from an inability to generalize skills. "I may do fine where I am but could I make it somewhere else?" Jobs are not looked on as opportunities to demonstrate particular skills but as self-definition.

Moving on because it is time is a carefully thought out and calculated decision. It involves preparation, planning and deliberate, systematic action. This is contrary to the operational mode of the ACoA, who operates best under pressure and in crisis.

ACoAs change jobs when circumstances intervene. Getting fired brings the same devastation for ACoAs as it does for others. Rejection — regardless of whether the job was worth having — brings up insecurities and people respond with either depression, which debilitates, or anger, which energizes. ACoAs are less prone than others to be able to use anger on their own behalf. It has been such a destructive force in the past that it is hard to harness it and make it useful. The knowledge of how to use anger and the freedom to see anger as being creative is not available to the ACoA.

Other circumstances, such as company moves, are managed extremely well by ACoAs. They are calm in the crisis and are able to do what needs to be done. Where others may fall apart in crisis and not be able to think clearly, ACoAs become energized and clear thinking. This is one benefit of the legacy of living from crisis to crisis in childhood.

12
Developing Healthy Workplace Relationships

would encourage you to begin thinking in terms of how to make things different. You can dwell forever on the pain. It is important to take a very good look at your issues, bring them out, chew them up, spit them out, know that they'll come up again from time to time and go on. You need to dwell on how you're going to make things different, what you're going to do to feel different in practical kinds of ways. What follows is a practical list.

Know Your Performance Style

Either accept it and work with it, or work to change it.

Many of you learned to do things under pressure because that was your life experience. You went from crisis to crisis. Nobody taught you how to do things systematically. Nobody said, "You need to spend an hour a night on your homework." So when you were in school, for example, if you got your paper in at all, you did it the night before. And now you have a deadline at work; even if you have had plenty of lead time, you probably do the job the night before. Then you come down on yourself, thinking there's something wrong with you because you always leave things until the last minute.

Leaving things until the last minute may be the way you work best. So rather than decide there's something wrong with you, recognize that this is the way you perform. Accept it!

If you have a history of getting things done when they're supposed to be done, don't automatically decide that you're doing it the wrong way. Know your performance style. It is important to know that about yourself. Different people operate differently and your early experiences may have taught you to operate best under pressure. It may have become your performance style. Concern yourself with it only if it's not working for you. Don't fix what's working. "If it ain't broke, don't fix it."

Be Aware Of Your Priorities And Live By Them

Not rigidly, but mindfully. ACoAs tend to give everything equal priority. Getting the wash done has the same priority as, say, filing your income tax. Life consists of many chores, obligations and projects. If each one has equal priority, it is very easy to become overwhelmed by all of them. Not everything has to be done immediately but some things do. Not everything has to be completed immediately but rather just held to manageable levels. If prioritizing is one of your difficult areas, you may need help with it.

The first thing you need to do is make a list of the things you have to do and give them a 1, 2 or 3 priority. If you have trouble doing this, ask your boss what needs to be done and when.

If you have time when you have completed the 1s, then do some of the 2s. Make this list every day. It will help to give you a handle on things. Otherwise, it is too easy to feel overwhelmed and to panic. Those feelings take a lot of energy and will drain you to the point where you are only able to accomplish very little and that feeds the panic.

Discover Your Limitations
And Live Realistically Within Them

You cannot do everything. We all have limitations. It is important to know that recognizing your limitations is not a way to put yourself down. Rather, it is a way to set realistic parameters to your work life. Become aware of your assets and respect them. You may not be able to feel good about them but you can be cognizant of them.

Be sure of your job description. It should be in writing. That way, you can know what your employer expects of you and you can determine what is reasonable to expect of yourself. If the demands on you are far different from your job description, it is important for you to find out what that means.

With a sense of your limitations, both personal and in terms of your job, you can then do some realistic goal setting. You can then define some parameters and become more secure in your work life. You can determine your direction and begin to develop a systematic way to get there.

Practice A Stress-Reducing Discipline Daily

This is absolutely essential.

Since so many of you are drawn to high stress occupations, it is very important to find ways of managing stress. A relaxation technique such as meditation or self-hypnosis, practiced on a daily basis, should become part of your lifestyle. If you don't practice it on a daily basis and it does not become a habit, you will not be able to draw on it when you need it.

Not only is this useful for reducing stress, it will help you to be more creative. Ideas that have no room to surface in a flooded mind or in a mind that is being outer-directed can come to the fore during meditation.

Many of the stress-related illnesses that you are prone to can be minimized, if not avoided entirely.

Separate The Being From The Doing

It's a complicated idea. What happens is that when someone criticizes your work, you take it as a criticism of yourself.

A counselor came in to see me, devastated because a woman said, "I am leaving your therapy group because I can get the same stuff from Al-Anon." The counselor began by defending himself. "You know," he said, "I've been a therapist for ten years and this hasn't happened to me before. I know I'm competent."

These are his words but not his feelings. He didn't react to her in terms of his competence. If he had reacted to her in terms of his competence, then he could have explored with her what it was about the group experience that she found lacking and learn from it.

What he reacted to instead was from an earlier time. What he heard was his father saying, "You'll never amount to anything." We had to address what went on in his self-esteem first in order for him to learn and change in the doing. When he recognized that the tape he was playing in his head was old and not accurate, he could then separate from it and look at the criticism in a new light. This happens over and over. Be careful, when someone criticizes you for what you do, that you take a look at it in terms of what you have done, not in terms of who you are. And if they criticize you in terms of who you are, then it is important for you to assess carefully whether or not this is a work situation that is beneficial for you to be in. None of us needs to be in a situation where our person is being judged.

Build In Time For Yourself

It is essential for you to have elements in your life other than work. Family, friends, hobbies and the like need to be part of your life.

If work is your whole life and the only place where your needs are met, you put yourself at risk. The loss of a job, a new boss who is difficult to work with or job dissatisfaction will be far more devastating than if you have other interests. Your entire identity should not be defined by your occupation. Loss of job need not be equated with loss of self if you take proper safeguards.

Building in time for yourself can also mean creating "nonproductive" time. Taking a bath, reading a novel, going for a walk, listening to music, riding a bike — these all fall into that category. Build this time in on a daily basis. Put it in ink on your daily calendar and be as conscientious to the self-commitment as you are to your commitment to others.

Learn What Is Appropriate And What Is Inappropriate To Share In The Work Setting

Though you feel close to others whom you work with, this does not mean that it is appropriate to tell them personal things. ACoAs, because of the boundary issues, tend to confuse this. An employer who comes to me for supervision asked my assessment of someone she had just interviewed. "You know, I really want to hire her, but during our interview she said, 'If I appear a little nervous it's because I just came from my doctor and he says I may have herpes.' "

That information was inappropriate to share with a potential employer. It started the employer questioning what the potential employee is going to share and what she is not going to share on the job. "I'm going to be sending this individual into schools. She's going to be developing relationships in those schools, and I'm concerned about what she will say."

It is not a good idea to share your fears and concerns with your employer. No matter how good the relationship is, your employer has got to be concerned about your job performance if you tell her how panicked you are that you won't be able to make it financially after the divorce, how you have had three sleepless nights in a row because your son comes in very late and very drunk. Your employer may care about you and your well-being, but that is not the relationship where disclosure of this nature is in your best interest.

Learn To Leave The Fantasy Out Of The Workplace. Learn How To Realistically Assess What Is Happening

It goes something like this: Because it's very easy for you, you get caught up in the fantasy. You need to assess realistically when your boss says, "I know I didn't give you the raise I promised, but in six months things are really gonna change," or, "I know the office is not what it's supposed to be but when we expand . . ." Be really careful about how easily you get sucked into this kind of stuff. "I am asking you now to take on this additional responsibility but it's not permanent." Watch it. Watch it.

Wishing doesn't make it so. It didn't when you were a child and it doesn't now. The difference is that as a child you had few options. As an adult you're in a different position. You can set a deadline for yourself. You can discover what control you have over seeing that desired changes occur. Then you live in the real world and take charge of yourself regardless of what flights of fancy are going on around you.

Don't Guess. Check Things Out

Guessing is one of the things you learned to do best as a child. You never learned to check things out; you never learned to ask. You never learned to question. But you really need to check things out. Things may not be as they appear because you're seeing them only from your personal frame of reference, so it's very important to ask if you're not sure. If you decide that somebody is angry with you, ask why. It may be important for you to know. And who knows? It might not even have anything to do with you.

A man who came to see me was very disturbed because someone was no longer saying hello to him in the morning. He couldn't figure out what he had done to offend this person and didn't know how to handle it. "What do I do about it? Do I confront him? Do I ignore him? Do I let it go? I'm lost and I don't want to make things worse."

"Are you the only one he's not saying good morning to?" I asked. He thought for a minute and then said, "Come to think of it, he's not greeting anybody."

The possibility is very strong that it may not have to do with you. It may have to do with him. Checking things out quite often takes the sting out of them. It helps you to begin to look at things realistically. Workplace rumors need to be checked out. Somehow, the walls have ears, but quite often the ears are clogged.

Mary, after a week of near desperation, finally went to her boss with a rumor she had heard. "I hear through the grapevine that you are looking to replace me and I thought I was doing a good job." She struggled to hold back the tears.

"I was hoping to save this announcement for the staff meeting and surprise you," he replied. "Your promotion has come through. Congratulations."

Before you approach your boss or co-workers, it is a good idea to check things out with a person or support group who cares about your best interest. You may need help in determining the appropriateness and style of presentation.

Although different circumstances may call for different strategies, the principle remains the same. Check things out. Don't guess.

Over-Reaction Is Historical. Learn To Separate The History From The Moment

If you find that something is really making you nuts, it probably doesn't have to do with the given situation. It probably relates back to something that happened in your childhood and the person in question has become someone else to you. It is important before you act or react on the basis of that, to figure out who that person is.

June's boss called her and said, "I need to see you. I have some bad news."

June panicked. "Oh my God! What have I done! What is going to happen to me? How can I cover myself? The panic was overwhelming. By the time I got to his office I was a basket case. He took one look at me and realized he had alarmed me. 'I'm sorry,' he said, 'The problem has nothing to do with you. I just need your input on how to explain to the staff that I'm not going to be able to offer the salary increases that I had projected.' " Her over-reaction was a direct result of her childhood. Anything that went wrong became her responsibility to fix, regardless of whether she had any part in its going wrong or whether she had any idea of how to fix it.

13
Finding The Right Job For You

Part of your growth may involve realizing that the job you hold may not be the right job for you. It is important to recognize that changing jobs involves a process. It is the same process for everyone, regardless of whether or not they grew up in a dysfunctional family. There are four steps in the process that ACoAs may not be aware of.

1. Prepare an up-to-date resume, whether or not you are satisfied with your present employment. This will give you an opportunity to explore whatever may come along and interest you — even tangentially. If you do not know how to prepare a resume, pick up a book on the subject and follow those guidelines. Nobody automatically knows how to do it until they have done it the first time. Have someone you trust look it over for typos or additional thoughts.
2. Take an interest inventory to see where your interests lie.
3. Take some aptitude tests and see where your potential lies.
4. Take a personality profile to find out your interactive style.

You may or may not be suited for the work you are doing and may be very confused as to what to do about it. Defining yourself by the opinions of others and trying to accept them as your own is most perplexing.

Taking stock of yourself in the ways listed above will give you an objective assessment of your ideal work profile and then you can explore the options. There are some good books on this subject. *What Color Is Your Parachute?* is among the most readable.

Learn about the process of job change and try to set up an orderly system for yourself — step by step — with a reasonable time frame.

You may feel that others have the edge when it comes to parenting and intimate relationships because they may have had good role models, but in the marketplace, as uneasy and insecure as you feel, you have the better survival skills. Those skills are a great leveler.

14
ACoAs As Counseling Professionals

CoAs make fine counseling professionals. Indeed many ACoAs, as we have seen, are involved in the field. This discussion does not relate to inadequacy on their part but rather the pitfalls many experience at work as counselors. It relates to their self-feelings and how they get in the way of feeling good about the job they do.

Children of alcoholics have very well-developed gut responses. This is a survival skill they learn as children. Words are not as meaningful to them as they are to other people. They can get their clues not only from the words but from a variety of other sources. They are able to gain a sense of what their client is feeling and where their client is at without going into lengthy descriptions which very often get in the way of knowing what is really going on. Since these gut reactions are so basic as to be almost instinctual, it is difficult to explain how you know. Counseling is one area where identification with childhood trauma can add to one's expertise — unfortunate, but true.

Children Of Alcoholics Very Often
See Themselves As Frauds

It is not unusual for the ACoA counselor to believe that he or she is a fraud. It has far more to do with self-feelings than with performance.

Someone I supervise came to me with this issue not too long ago. "How can I help my clients build their self-esteem if I struggle with that myself?" he said.

The idea that unless all of your personal issues are resolved, you are counseling under false pretenses would mean that no one would be qualified to be a counselor. If your client's issue is your own *current* struggle, you may need to refer him or her to someone else. Counselors need to be human and not being finished is a part of being human.

Most of us, from time to time, when faced with new situations that involve the demonstration of confidence feel like little kids playing grown-up. It is that child within us that has the performance anxiety.

The fear of the ACoA is deeper, and each workplace job performance assessment brings it up all over again. "How long will it be until they discover I've been fooling them into believing that I know what I'm doing?" This leaves the ACoA in a continual state of stress.

Adult Children Of Alcoholics Tend To Over-Identify
With And Become Over-Invested In Their Clients

This is a boundary issue that relates directly back to childhood. It was impossible to know where your needs and feelings ended and someone else's began. It was impossible to know who was the parent and who was the child. To what degree were you supposed to make it right for everyone else? How could you know what was your problem and what was somebody else's? It's very easy to become overly concerned with your clients as well.

It is not to the client's benefit to bring concerns about him or her home with you night after night. It does not improve your skill as a counselor not to be able to leave your clients behind. The client will not know the difference but you will propel yourself toward burnout. You are not your client. Your client's growth is not a measure of your personal growth. The parameters need to be made clear and one of the ways to make them clear is to work with the client during the time that you are working with the client and let that be that. If supervision is necessary, that is something else again, but supervision is formally structured. When you leave your place of work, you leave it. You may have to fight your mind for a while in order to accomplish this but it may be the difference between your remaining in the field and your getting burned out. Taking your work home with you does not make you a better counselor.

The discussion in a supervision group was on working with families in which a family member has committed suicide. As the discussion went on, one of the clinicians in the group looked more and more depressed. When I asked him what was going on with him, he said, "The discussion is getting to me. This is a very serious problem area for me. I find that I take on my client's issues like lint and I am unable to pick them off. I know *how* to be different. I know the professional discipline that it takes. I know the principles of detachment. I know how to replace one thought with another. I know that I am not all-powerful and cannot fix everything for everybody. None of that knowledge seems to do me any good. What do you suppose this means?"

"It's certainly a boundary issue for you," I said. "Your parents never respected your boundaries. They constantly humiliated you in public. They took credit for whatever you did that was good and wonderful. They never let you be separate from them. They never let you develop and separate yourself as a person. I suspect that this is a reason why you're going to be the opposite of your parents. You are so angry at your parents and so critical of your parents that whatever they say, whatever they do, however they behave, there is a red flag saying 'I will behave the opposite way.' Since they were always angry, you never allow yourself to be angry. Since they were always out of control, you always need to maintain control.

"I suspect they also had no compassion for other human beings. They certainly had no compassion or sensitivity toward what you were feeling and certainly did not spend time and demonstrate concern for what was going on with you. Here again, you have decided to be the opposite of them. In so doing you have become over-involved. You are too caring."

It is the extremes with which we must concern ourselves. Because your parents were not caring does not mean that you need to be all-consumed with caring. It does mean that you have to move a little bit more toward their position. The ideal for both you and your parents is to be more centered. The reality is that for your own growth, you need, in some ways, to be more like them.

ACoAs Need To Have Everyone Like Them.
They Seek Approval Not Only From Their Supervisors
And Peers But Also From Those They Serve

This is another area that can become burdensome for you. Clients will simply not like you all the time. It is part of your responsibility to do and say things that they do not like. They cannot separate your words from your person and they will get angry at you. This goes with the territory. You need to be very careful not to carry this response around with you. The important thing is that your clients hear and do the things that are to their benefit. The important thing is the positive movement toward growth.

A client of mine called me from a rehab center. She was very angry with me. She said, "You told me I would not have a great deal of difficulty with withdrawal and I had a terrible time." My response was, "That was because I didn't realize what bad shape you were in."

She began to laugh. I did not have to take on her anger. I did not have to defend myself. I was able to affect her getting the help that she requires. That is my job. That is my goal. If she needs someone to blame when she is angry, so be it. The blaming will not last long. It will stop when she begins to feel better. But her interests are my interests. It's very hard to separate that out if you are looking for your client's approval.

I suggest that if you need to seek approval — and we all do to one degree or another — you seek it from people who are in at least as good shape as you are. If your clients are in at least as good shape as you are, you may want to reconsider what you are doing for a living.

Adult Children Of Alcoholics Avoid Conflict

It is certainly understandable that if you grew up in a home where there was always conflict and never resolution, you would back away from it. If you grew up in a home where you were afraid, when anger was expressed, that either you would be hurt or that someone else would be hurt or that you would be invisible or that someone else would be rejected — it is not difficult to see why you would discourage this kind of behavior.

An aspect that you have to look at critically is whether or not you yourself know how to resolve conflict. It is absolutely essential not only in your personal life but in your work life that you develop the necessary tools to deal with working through and resolving conflict.

Adult Children Of Alcoholics
Have Difficulty Making Referrals

The difficulty in making referrals comes from fear of being found out. If you make a referral, the fear is that others will discover that you are incompetent. They will learn that you could not work with this client, that you did not have the necessary skills to work with this client. You don't want people to know your limitations. The reality is that we all have limitations and the idea is not to try to hide them but to recognize them. In recognizing that there are others who are more skilled with certain clients than we are, we better serve our clients. We cannot be specialists in all areas. We cannot relate to all the people who come to see us. It is not possible nor is it desirable. "I cannot help you but I can help you find somebody who can" is a statement of competence.

ACoAs Are Impatient With Stuck Clients

This results from self-judgment, in part, and also a judgment of the client. The self-judgment is, "If I were a better clinician, my client would not get stuck. Therefore, the inability of my client to move at this time is a negative reflection on me."

The other part of it is a counter-transference issue with your client. "I was where you are and I got through it, I got by it, I did what I had to do. Why can't you?"

There may be two realities here. One may be that your client only looks stuck. Sometimes people need time to consolidate their learning. Sometimes people need to take a breather before they move on and make new decisions. Sometimes clients remain stuck so that they don't have to make the change that is so terrifying to them.

The other aspect is that there may be something you could be doing for your client that you are not doing. Believing that it is an inadequacy in you that causes your client to be stuck will get in the way of your asking a supervisor or a fellow counselor for some thoughts on what they would do if they were in this position.

"My client is stuck" and "I must fix" are not equivalent statements.

Many Look For A Treatment Road Map

Many want to know before they begin with a client just exactly what to do, how to take it, where to take it, how long it will take, what the best approach to take is, what one should not do, and so on. It's not unusual to get this request for guidance. Essentially it's asking for a road map through treatment. It's not a whole lot different from the road map that many ACoAs want for their lives. "Tell me what to do. Tell me how to handle myself. Tell me if I am doing the right thing. Tell me if I am doing the wrong thing. Is this a good decision to make? Is this a poor decision to make?" This difficulty and this need for structure, order and direction are legacies from childhood. Because there was no foundation on which to build, there is a great deal of insecurity left in deciding what the correct road to take is.

Those of us who train counselors would be disrespectful in giving you a treatment road map. There is no treatment road map just as there is no life road map. There are the things that work and the things that don't work. There are the things one tries out that work successfully, and there are things one tests that don't work out so successfully. It is important to be able to help your client discover options and alternatives, to help your client be aware of the possible consequences of exploring each one of these options and alternatives. If this is what you are truly asking, if this is what you are really looking for, it is different from looking for a road map. It is saying, "What are the different courses this treatment could take? What are the possibilities that I need to be mindful of before I begin? What are my goals and what are my client's goals?" Those are legitimate questions. Those are important questions. Those questions may need to be asked.

ACoAs Who Are Clinicians Are Poor Stress Managers

Being stressed has been the natural order of things. You grew up in a stress-filled household. It was what you knew. It was the way you felt all the time. As a result, when you are stressed in the workplace, you are not necessarily aware of it. Working with clients is a very difficult, highly stressful situation. You do not have an opportunity to relax; you do not have an opportunity to give anyone less than your full attention. If you are relaxing or if you are giving your client less than your full attention, you are not doing your job. Therefore, by definition, you are in a highly stressful situation. This isn't to say that it cannot be really satisfying — maybe you prefer to work this way. What it does say is that it is important for you to recognize that this stress must be managed. It is important for you to recognize that you must take relief from the stress. It is important that you develop the means to do so.

ACoAs Who Are Clinicians
Deny Their Own Counter-Transference

Counter-transference somehow is a dirty word. Clinicians are not supposed to counter-transfer. Clients are supposed to transfer but clinicians are not supposed to counter-transfer. Therefore, a clinician who has a counter-transference reaction to a client is less than perfect. So since ACoAs who are clinicians feel they have to be perfect, they will tend to deny their own counter-transference. It is not possible for you not to be drawn to a child you would like to take home. It is not possible for you not to be furious at someone who behaves like someone in your life who abused you. It is sometimes not possible for you not to be sexually drawn to a client. This is simply the way it is. Admitting it to yourself means that you can get a handle on it. Sometimes it's not serious. Sometimes your awareness of your response to this client means it will not get in your way.

Sometimes a reaction is so powerful that it becomes necessary for you to refer that client to somebody else. This is not a reflection on you. If it happens consistently, you may want to take a good look at the matter. It is not useful for you to deny it. The transference of the client to the counselor is a very useful one for the ACoA. It is not harmful for the clinician to be proud of the client's growth and progress. This pride is certainly a parental pride. It feels good and it is not at all harmful to the client. If it goes much further than that, you need to be careful. I know I had to stop seeing young children. My counter-transference reaction to them was too great. I wanted to bring all of them home with me. I wanted to take care of them. They had in fact become mine. This was not useful or beneficial to them, nor was it useful or beneficial to me.

ACoAs Who Are Clinicians
Tend Not To Limit Their Caseloads

You are the one in the agency who will take on that additional case. You are the one they can always be sure will take one more.

This has to do with your inability to say No. This has to do with your not recognizing when you are being exploited.

It is very important that you recognize just how many clients it is appropriate for you to handle and at what point it is a good idea for you to say No. Check around. Don't do this within your own agency; if you are being exploited there is a very good chance that others are being exploited too. Check with people who work in other places and feel comfortable with their workload. See if they are carrying as many clients as you are. See how their case management is worked out. Where in your day is time built in for the paperwork that piles up way over your head? Where is time built in for you to return phone calls? This is all part of your job description. If you are seeing clients from the minute you walk in until the minute you leave and then have to do this work on your own, your caseload is inappropriate. It is exploitive. You must take steps to balance the situation.

This may be a good opportunity to check yourself and find out if you are propelling toward burnout. The counselor who does not take careful precautions will not last. Balance is the goal.

The Balance/Burnout Checklist For Counselors

Emotional Health

1. How much time do you spend worrying about your clients and their problems?
2. Are there moments when you believe your work situation is hopeless and that you cannot help anyone?
3. Do you have strong mood swings and feelings about your clients? Your work? Your own family and friends?
4. How often do you blame the administration, your colleagues or your clients for your own bad feelings?
5. Would your life be fine if only staff and clients behaved differently?
6. How often do you feel lonely? When you're with others — or by yourself?
7. Do you ever question your own sanity? Lose control?
8. When does your own behavior make you feel ashamed?
9. Are you often fearful?
10. Is work more important than your family and/or social life?
11. How do you control your anger and frustration?
12. What makes you feel responsible for the behavior of others?
13. Do you feel guilty about your work some of the time?

14. Do you feel overwhelmed by your working responsibilities?
15. Are you becoming more sensitive to and more critical of others at home and at work?

Physical Health

1. How are your sleeping habits being affected? Toss and turn? Escape by sleeping long hours?
2. What physical symptoms of illness in yourself have you noticed? Headaches? Nausea? "Knot" in the stomach? Exhaustion? Agitation? Backaches? Pains in the neck?
3. How have your eating habits changed?
4. Have you been involved in physical violence in your home or with friends?
5. How has your sexual life changed?

Social Health

1. How is your concentration on your work affecting your daily life? Working overtime? Not spending time with family and friends? Not taking time for recreation?
2. Do you spend much of your time reacting to crises and feeling your life is not your own?
3. Has life become so very serious that you have lost your sense of humor?
4. Do you find yourself forgetting things? Losing things? Having minor accidents?
5. Do you spend your free time during the working day talking about clients?
6. Do you have your clients check in with you regularly so that you may monitor their behavior?
7. How do you overprotect your clients?
8. What responsibilities have you given up in your family so that you may continue to concentrate on work?
9. How have you let work interfere with social plans?
10. Do you ever feel unappreciated at work?
11. Do you sometimes think your clients cannot survive without your good advice?
12. How do you let clients affect your own feelings? Your behavior?
13. Do you ever threaten clients or intimidate them in confrontations? Are you ever sarcastic?

Reprinted with permission from Hazelden: *Manual for the Family Program for Professionals*. Original concept by Terry Williams & Ruth Friedman.

15
Thoughts For Employee Assistance Programs

n Employee Assistance Program is an ideal route to draw ACoAs into the treatment they need. Because people spend a large portion of their lives in the workplace, it is here, surrounded by colleagues who do not necessarily have the personal investment in the working relationship, that ACoA behavior can be perceived and addressed — for the good of both the individual and the company. There are no losers when the ACoA gets the care he or she needs and deserves.

For the individual this care can often serve as the deterrent from progressing into alcoholism or other forms of substance abuse.

As Cindy tells us:

> Five years ago, frightened by my own increased drinking, worried about the impact of alcoholism on another generation and supported by therapy, I made a decision to stop drinking and to face the personal and family problems related to multi-generational alcoholism that I had avoided and denied. The decision to take charge of my life and then to fulfill the Serenity Prayer has increasingly contributed to an understanding of my motivations and therefore a lessening of the necessity for me to work out my unresolved conflicts through the work itself.

117

It can help to quiet what Mark called "the inner voice of failure" that sabotages the personal as well as the professional life.

Michael, the manager of an EAP for a large high-tech research company, describes the benefits for the company as well as for the individual.

> In almost every case adult children of alcoholics respond well to counseling . . . The degree of isolation, support systems, etcetera, determines the length of treatment. The prognosis for these clients is excellent once they are treated.

In other words, when you begin to address the issues of the ACoA in the workplace, you begin to address the billions of dollars lost through poor job performance, lost sales, on-the-job accidents, absence from work, medical costs, and the costs of hiring and training new personnel.

But it was the religious counselor who most poignantly described the benefits of ACoA treatment:

> God made you. It's okay to be you. It's even okay to love yourself. In fact, the more you can love yourself, the easier it is for you to help others.

This ideal exists in all relationships. It is a workplace goal as well as a personal goal. It is a direction for us all to follow.

Some companies are in a position to offer an educational series to their employees. The components of an educational series on and for adult children of alcoholics could be the following.

Week One: An Overview — Adult Children Of Alcoholics

The first week is designed to include general information pertaining to ACoAs. This seminar introduces the education series and describes the content and focus of the seven following weeks.

Objectives

Participants will learn of the cost of alcoholism and related problems to their company.

Participants will become familiar with the research, literature and experiences of the largest population of people affected by alcoholism.

Participants may identify themselves as belonging to this population.

Participants will have the opportunity to ask questions and receive clarification on individual problems and concerns, and to assess whether the education will be of further help.

Week Two: The Childhood Experience

This seminar introduces the "family disease" concept. The interpersonal dynamics of the alcoholic family are explained. The leader discusses early perceptions of reality and the coping mechanisms children of alcoholics developed for survival.

Objectives

Participants will become aware of the progressive processes of the family disease.

Participants will become aware of how these family dynamics can be replayed in the workplace.

Participants will become familiar with how a functional family system deals with problem solving, expression of emotions, and communication.

Week Three: Adaptation To Alcoholism

This seminar focuses on the roles assumed by family members and how these roles are both functional and dysfunctional in childhood and adulthood. This lecture stresses the need for ACoAs to identify how roles serve as a protective defense from emotional turmoil as well as provide the ACoA with a sense of self based on what they do versus who they are and how they feel. This seminar includes a discussion on conditional versus unconditional love.

Objectives

Participants will become familiar with various roles assumed in alcoholic families and identify how various roles serve in maintaining survival, reducing stress, and creating a sense of stability for the ACoA.

Participants will discuss the strengths and weaknesses implied in various roles, what the advantages and disadvantages were, and what emotions the roles repressed.

Participants will identify how the alcoholic and co-dependent parents responded conditionally to various role behaviors versus responding unconditionally to the whole child.

Week Four: Adult Traits And Characteristics

Discussion of adult traits and characteristics as determined by researchers. This seminar focuses on problems experienced by ACoAs and how these problems have roots in the family history of alcoholism. The messages and distorted perceptions internalized throughout childhood in an alcoholic environment are examined.

Objectives

Participants will become aware of the manifestations of the employee's isolation in the workplace.

Participants will learn how these internalized overt or covert messages interfere with employee's present functioning.

Participants will develop strategies toward change.

Week Five: Self-Help For ACoAs

This seminar uses a broad-based definition of self-help to assist the ACoA in utilizing resources to aid in recovery. The traditional programs of self-help such as AA, Al-Anon and ACoA are discussed. The participants are also exposed to the help available through education and various community resources. Various forms of therapy are discussed.

Objectives

Participants will become aware of available recovery programs.

Participants will utilize a variety of resources to help with various needs.

Week Six: Intimacy

This seminar will, through lecture, film, discussion, and group exercises, show how living with alcoholism can interfere with the ability to experience intimacy. The goal of this seminar is to define intimacy and discuss the components of healthy relationships.

Objective

Participants will discover how problems of intimacy can affect workplace behavior.

Week Seven: The Recovery Process

The seminar focuses on the recovery process. Needs and problems encountered during various stages of recovery are discussed. The behavioral, cognitive and emotional changes experienced in recovery, and how change occurs are highlighted.

Objective

Participants will learn to understand recovery as a process.

ACoA Warning Signs: A Checklist For EAPs

Just as it takes time to get to know someone, it takes time to perceive the effects of an undiagnosed ACoA on the job. Here are some of the most important manifestations of ACoAs creating difficulties for themselves on the job:

- Procrastination
- Perfectionism
- Indecisiveness
- Impulsiveness in decision-making
- Inconsistent productivity
- Too many questions
- No questions at all
- Difficulty in accepting compliments
- Constant approval-seeking
- Often working very late
- High absenteeism
- Over-involvement with other employees' personal problems
- Apparent disregard for other employees' feelings
- Assuming responsibility for other people's mistakes
- Lack of initiative
- Frequent emotional outbursts
- No display of emotions at all
- Too much discussion of personal life
- No apparent life outside of work.

The reader will see that many of the items on this list form pairs. The ACoA will often flip-flop from one extreme to the other — productivity is a case in point.

But it's important to note that these manifestations vary, depending on the nature of the workplace and that this list is incomplete. Further research is required to determine whether ACoAs create stress on the job, how they respond to it when it does occur, and what effect this has on their fellow employees.

Crisis Counseling For ACoAs: A Checklist For EAPs

1. *Referred for job performance problems.*
   Look first for signs of substance abuse.
2. *Absenteeism due to illness.*
   Check for burnout or substance abuse.
3. *Problems with peers and supervisors.*
   Look for playing out of alcohol family system.
4. *Problems with family.*
   Look for substance abuse or other compulsive behaviors in
      self, spouse or children.
   Look for lack of understanding of how to solve the problem.
5. *Problems with intimacy.*
   Look for fears of abandonment.
   Look for substance abuse in lover.
   Look for lover within the organization and the relationship
      going bad.

CONCLUSION

The legacy of childhood clearly demonstrates itself in the workplace. This is true for everyone regardless of their background. Your history can either work for you or against you. You can decide to change or adapt. Once you have insight, you have choices.

Clinical practice clearly shows that ACoAs respond very quickly to treatment. They are eager for help and make very good use of tools gained in the counseling process.

In the substance-abuse field, we talk in terms of prevention, intervention, and treatment.

Prevention lies in education. "I feel this way because of part of my childhood experience. I behave this way because of part of my childhood experience."

Intervention lies in breaking the cycle. "I need to make changes because what I'm doing and feeling is not working for me."

Treatment is the development of new messages:

I am a person of worth.

I can demonstrate it.

I can feel it.

I can make choices.

I can work for you and not lose me.

I can grow with the organization and not leave me behind.

I will take me with me.

The EAP counselor who works with the ACoA participates in an exciting growth process. The shift from me (the object) to I (the subject) creates an energy that can be productive for all concerned.

The value of the ACoA in the workplace gets clearer and clearer. Recognition of the signs of ACoA issues as they surface, and responding quickly and appropriately to them will, in both the long and short run, result in maintaining superior workers and greatly reduce the losses due to burnout, physical problems, substance abuse, and impulsive job changes. It is in the economic best interest of companies to be responsive. It is to the advantage of all — not just ACoAs, but their colleagues as well — to address these issues as they arise and not wait until they reach bitter fruition. The workplace itself will become a more productive and healthier environment.

BIBLIOGRAPHY

"Employee Assistance Programs: Blending Performance-Oriented and Humanitarian Ideologies to Assist Emotionally Disturbed Employees." *Research in Community and Mental Health,* 1984, Vol. 4, pp. 245-259.

Podolsky, Doug M., "RTI Report: Economic Costs of Alcohol Abuse and Alcoholism." *Alcohol Health and Research World,* Winter 1984/ 1985, pp. 34-35.

"A Retrospective Study of Similarities and Differences Between Men and Women Employees in a Job-Based Alcoholism Program: 1976-1977." *Journal of Drug Issues,* 1981, Vol. 11, pp. 233-262.

Shealey, Tom. "Your Secret Signals." *Prevention,* September 1985, Vol. 37, no. 9, pp. 68-72.

Sonnenstuhl, William J. "Understanding EAP Self-Referral: Toward a Social Network Approach." *Contemporary Drug Problems,* Summer 1982, pp. 269-293.

Steele, Paul D., and Robert L. Hubbard. "Management Styles, Perceptions of Substance Abuse and Employee Assistance Programs in Organizations." *The Journal of Applied Behavioral Science,* 1985, Vol. 21, no. 3, pp. 271-286.

Trice, Harrison M. "Employee Assistance Programs: Where Do We Stand in 1983?" *Journal of Psychiatric Treatment and Evaluation,* 1983, Vol. 5, pp. 521-552.

Trice, Harrison M., and Janice M. Beyer. "A Databased Examination of Selection Bias in the Evaluation of Job-Based Alcoholism Program." *Alcoholism: Clinical and Experimental Research,* Fall 1981, Vol. 5, no. 4, pp. 489-496.

"Work-Related Outcomes of the Constructive Confrontation Strategy in a Job-Based Alcoholism Program." *Journal of Studies on Alcohol,* September 1984, Vol. 45, no. 5, pp. 393-404.

Other Books by Janet G. Woititz

Adult Children Of Alcoholics

There are some 28 million children of alcoholics living in the United States. This heritage has followed all of them into adulthood. What they need is basic information to sort out the effects of alcoholism in their lives. Dr. Woititz' book is the first to provide this crucial material.

ISBN 0-932194-15-X   (Soft cover 5½x8½ 106 pg.)
Code 415X $6.95

Marriage On The Rocks

What is a wife to do when "he" drinks too much? . . . When the marriage is "on the rocks?" Sensitive, thoughtful, compassionate advice is offered for the wife living with and loving an alcoholic husband. The time for change is now . . . the tools for change are here.

ISBN 0-932194-17-6   (Soft cover 5½x8½ 147 pg.)
Code 4176 .... $6.95

Struggle For Intimacy

This book is must reading for everyone wanting more from their intimate relationships with spouses, lovers, friends and family. The "struggle" doesn't have to be quite so tough . . . and this book will show you how to get what you want from your relationships.

ISBN 0-932194-25-7   (Soft cover 5½x8½ 101 pg.)
Code 4257 .... $6.95

Healing Your Sexual Self

How can you break through the aftermath of sexual abuse and enter into healthy relationships? In this book, Dr. Woititz explains in clear and direct language that the process begins with recognizing that *something has gone wrong* and how to deal with your recovery.

ISBN 1-55874-018-X   (Soft cover 5½x8½ 138 pg.)
Code 018X $7.95

Books from . . .
Health Communications

AFTER THE TEARS: *Reclaiming The Personal Losses of Childhood*
Jane Middelton-Moz and Lorie Dwinnel
Your lost childhood must be grieved in order for you to recapture your self-worth and enjoyment of life. This book will show you how.
ISBN 0-932194-36-2 $7.95

HEALING YOUR SEXUAL SELF
Janet Woititz
How can you break through the aftermath of sexual abuse and enter into healthy relationships? Survivors are shown how to recognize the problem and deal effectively with it.
ISBN 1-55874-018-X $7.95

RECOVERY FROM RESCUING
Jacqueline Castine
Effective psychological and spiritual principles teach you when to take charge, when to let go, and how to break the cycle of guilt and fear that keeps you in the responsibility trap. Mind-altering ideas and exercises will guide you to a more carefree life.
ISBN 1-55874-016-3 $7.95

ADDICTIVE RELATIONSHIPS: Reclaiming Your Boundaries
Joy Miller
We have given ourselves away to spouse, lover, children, friends or parents. By examining where we are, where we want to go and how to get there, we can reclaim our personal boundaries and the true love of ourselves.
ISBN 1-55874-003-1 $7.95

RECOVERY FROM CO-DEPENDENCY:
It's Never Too Late To Reclaim Your Childhood
Laurie Weiss, Jonathan B. Weiss
Having been brought up with life-repressing decisions, the adult child recognizes something isn't working. This book shows how to change decisions and live differently and fully.
ISBN 0-932194-85-0 $9.95

SHIPPING/HANDLING: All orders shipped UPS unless weight exceeds 200 lbs., special routing is requested, or delivery territory is outside continental U.S. Orders outside United States shipped either Air Parcel Post or Surface Parcel Post. Shipping and handling charges apply to all orders shipped whether UPS, Book Rate, Library Rate, Air or Surface Parcel Post or Common Carrier and will be charged as follows. Orders less than $25.00 in value add $2.00 minimum. Orders from $25.00 to $50.00 in value (after discount) add $2.50 minimum. Orders greater than $50.00 in value (after discount) add 6% of value. Orders greater than $25.00 outside United States add 15% of value. We are not responsible for loss or damage unless material is shipped UPS. Allow 3-5 weeks after receipt of order for delivery. Prices are subject to change without prior notice.

Enterprise Center, 3201 S.W. 15th Street,
Deerfield Beach, FL 33442
1-800-851-9100

Health Communications, Inc.

New Books . . .
from Health Communications

HEALING THE SHAME THAT BINDS YOU
John Bradshaw
Toxic shame is the core problem in our compulsions, co-dependencies and addictions. The author offers healing techniques to help release the shame that binds us.
ISBN 0-932194-86-9 $9.95

THE MIRACLE OF RECOVERY:
Healing For Addicts, Adult Children and Co-dependents
Sharon Wegscheider-Cruse
Beginning with recognizing oneself as a survivor, it is possible to move through risk and change to personal transformation.
ISBN 1-55874-024-4 $9.95

CHILDREN OF TRAUMA: *Rediscovering Your Discarded Self*
Jane Middelton-Moz
This beautiful book shows how to discover the source of past traumas and grieve them to grow into whole and complete adults.
ISBN 1-55874-014-7 $9.95

New Books on Spiritual Recovery . . .

LEARNING TO LIVE IN THE NOW: *6-Week Personal Plan To Recovery*
Ruth Fishel
The author gently introduces you step by step to the valuable healing tools of meditation, positive creative visualization and affirmations.
ISBN 0-932194-62-1 $7.95

CYCLES OF POWER: *A User's Guide To The Seven Seasons of Life*
Pamela Levin
This innovative book unveils the process of life as a cyclic pattern, providing strategies to use the seven seasons to regain power over your life.
ISBN 0-932194-75-3 $9.95

MESSAGES FROM ANNA: *Lessons in Living (Santa Claus, God and Love)*
Zoe Rankin
This is a quest for the meaning of "love." In a small Texas Gulf Coast town a wise 90-year-old woman named Anna shares her life messages.
ISBN 1-55874-013-9 $7.95

THE FLYING BOY: *Healing The Wounded Man*
John Lee
A man's journey to find his "true masculinity" and his way out of co-dependent and addictive relationships, this book is about feelings — losing them, finding them, expressing them.
ISBN 1-55874-006-6 $7.95

Enterprise Center, 3201 S.W. 15th Street,
Deerfield Beach, FL 33442
1-800-851-9100

Health Communications, Inc.